40 Murders and Mysteries Solved by Science

Larry Verstraete

Scholastic Canada Ltd.

Toronto New York London Auckland Sydney
Mexico City New Delhi Hong Kong Buenos Aires

For scientists and educators who stoke the fires of understanding
and imagination, casting dreams of future possibilities

Scholastic Canada Ltd.
604 King Street West, Toronto, Ontario M5V 1E1, Canada

Scholastic Inc.
557 Broadway, New York, NY 10012, USA

Scholastic Australia Pty Limited
PO Box 579, Gosford, NSW 2250, Australia

Scholastic New Zealand Limited
Private Bag 94407, Botany, Manukau 2163, New Zealand

Scholastic Children's Books
Euston House, 24 Eversholt Street, London NW1 1DB, UK

Library and Archives Canada Cataloguing in Publication
Verstraete, Larry
    Case files : 40 murders and mysteries solved by science / Larry Verstraete.

Includes index.
ISBN 978-1-4431-0000-7

    1. Forensic sciences--Juvenile literature. I. Title.

HV8073.8.V47 2011   j363.25   C2011-902067-X

6 5 4 3 2 1   Printed in Canada   121   11 12 13 14 15 16

TABLE OF CONTENTS

I keep six honest serving-men,
They taught me all I knew,
Their names are What and Why and When
and How and Where and Who
— Rudyard Kipling

INTRODUCTION

- Workers digging a ditch discover the skeleton of a girl wrapped in a carpet. Who is this nameless person? Can she be *identified?*

- A boy is viciously murdered. Other than an oily smear on his jacket, there is little evidence at the scene. Can the oily stain *prove* who committed the murder?

- Weathered bones are discovered buried in a field. There are two bodies, but the limbs are intertwined in a strange way and the lower legs of one are missing entirely. What happened to these two people? What is the *explanation?*

- A painting is up for sale. Some say it is a masterpiece. Others claim that it is a clever forgery. Which is it? Can the controversy be *resolved?*

This book contains stories about these and other perplexing cases that have been solved with the help of scientists. Like the questions asked above, the four chapters focus on different purposes or goals of science detection: *Identify, Prove, Explain* and *Resolve.*

The cases in each chapter range from crimes and suspicious deaths to lost ships and missing persons. The type of scientist involved varies, too. In some cases, entomologists — bug experts — are called for answers. Other times geologists who have knowledge about soil deposits are needed. Or it might be archeologists skilled in interpreting artifacts, or perhaps forensic anthropologists — bone specialists — who eventually solve the puzzle. In complex situations, more than one kind of scientist might be involved, each bringing different areas of expertise, each using different tools and methods.

Whatever the case, whatever the field of science, the process is much the same. Questions lead the way. Who did this? What happened? Where? How? Why? By gathering and analyzing evidence, by carefully deciphering the clues, scientists piece together answers. Often a hidden story emerges, a mystery unravels, and the case is solved.

CHAPTER 1
IDENTIFY

Introduction

On May 17, 2001, workers opened a grave on top of a small hill in Fairview Lawn Cemetery in Halifax, Nova Scotia. Below the dirt they found remnants of a coffin, a piece of wrist bone, and the crowns of three tiny baby teeth. After eight and a half decades in the damp, acidic soil, that was all that remained of a small child plucked from the icy waters of the Atlantic following the sinking of the ship *Titanic*.

The bones offered hope for two Canadian scientists, however. For Ryan Parr of Lakehead University in Thunder Bay, Ontario, and Alan Ruffman of Geomarine Associates Ltd. in Halifax, it was a chance to bring an end to a long-standing puzzle. Who was the child buried in the grave — *Titanic*'s "Unknown Child"?

In 1912, the *Titanic* had sunk off the coast of Newfoundland after striking an iceberg. Among the fifteen hundred victims was an unidentified baby boy. Four children on the *Titanic's* passenger list were close to the same age as the unknown child — Gosta Paulson, Eino Panula, Eugene Rice and Sidney Goodwin. But without survivors to identify the body, a match was impossible.

After exhuming the bones, Parr and Ruffman extracted

3

DNA from the teeth and compared it to DNA obtained from living relatives of the four children on the passenger list. A match was found to a relative of Eino Panula. The mystery was solved. Or so it appeared.

In 2007, the case was revisited. By then DNA extraction methods had improved, particularly in cases involving old bones. DNA tests for the Unknown Child were repeated. This time a different, more exact conclusion was reached. The Unknown Child was not Eino Panula, but Sidney Goodwin.

For Goodwin's relatives, the conclusion provided a small measure of closure. All other members of Sidney Goodwin's immediate family had been aboard the *Titanic*. In the tragedy, all eight had disappeared, their bodies never recovered. Now at least, the fate of one was known.

In this chapter, you will meet scientists on similar quests. Whether it is anthropologists trying to identify mysterious bones, marine archeologists who hope to locate a lost ship, or microbiologists who seek the origins of a strange illness, the approach and goals are much the same no matter the type of science. By isolating factors, by pinpointing what is truly unique and matching it to the evidence, these scientists unravel the clues that crack the case.

The Disturbing Case of the Skeleton in the Carpet

The flesh was gone; only bones remained. Who was this person buried in such a careless and callous manner?

The ramshackle, three-storey house in Cardiff, Wales, was under renovation when workmen, digging for a new sewer pipe, struck something strangely soft with their pickaxes. Buried under a garden wall was a roll of carpet tied up with an electrical cord. When the bundle was unwrapped, a human skeleton was revealed. The flesh was long gone, but a few scraps of clothing clung to the bones. A small skull was framed by a tangle of blond hair and, nearby, a pair of earrings.

Work on the house stopped. Police were called and by late afternoon the house at 29 Fitzhamon Embankment was converted into a crime scene. Tape was strung across doors. The yard was cordoned off. A large plastic tent was erected over the area and investigators scoured the yard for clues. It appeared as though someone had gone to a lot of trouble to hide the body and never intended it to be found. Just when, why and how the crime had happened, though, was anyone's guess. But the most important question on everyone's mind was, *Who was the person in the carpet?*

An army of scientific investigators was called. Among them was forensic entomologist Dr. Zakaria Erzinclioglu of Cambridge University. Erzinclioglu was sent soil and carpet samples along with insect and plant material from the ditch. His job was to use his knowledge of insect biology to help solve the crime. Erzinclioglu found large numbers of empty pupal cases, a sign that scuttle flies had once occupied the body's soft tissues. The flies had laid eggs, which later hatched to produce larvae. Still later, the larvae had pupated and entered a cocoon-like stage before shedding their protective casings and transforming into adults. Erzinclioglu also found wood lice that had been attracted to fungus growing on the bones. By determining their stages of growth and by comparing them to the growth of insects found in the surrounding soil, Erzinclioglu was able to estimate the time of death. The victim had died at least five years before.

Erzinclioglu's findings were confirmed when a sweatshirt found with the body was checked against dates from the manufacturer's records. The death had likely occurred between 1980 and 1984. With this information, detectives could narrow down the list of possible identities to people who had gone missing in this period of time.

The bones belonged to a female teenager around 163 centimetres tall.

Pathology professor Bernard Knight was also consulted. He was the medical specialist who would examine the body tissues and bones to find causes of injury or disease, and death. Knight measured the bones and examined them for distinctive features that would tell the victim's gender, age and size. The wideness of the pelvic bones, for example, indicated that the skeleton was female. By taking measurements of the major bones and analyzing their wear and the amount of calcium they contained, Knight was able to estimate her age and height. His conclusion: the bones belonged to a female teenager around 163 centimetres tall.

A day after the body's discovery, the skull was delivered to Dr. David Whittaker, a forensic dentist. He X-rayed the skull to check the root development of the girl's teeth. Then he removed one tooth and sliced it lengthwise for a closer look. Teeth, particularly molars, develop gradually, often reaching maturity late in adolescence or early adulthood. By examining the size and development of the roots, Whittaker was able to more closely establish the girl's age. The root structure, he concluded, was that of a fifteen-and-a-half-year-old. Scientists had now determined the girl's age, sex and approximate date of death. But more research was needed if they wanted to give the victim a name.

The skull was sent to two anthropologists at London's Natural History Museum, Dr. Christopher Stringer and Dr. Theya Molleson, who studied the origins, development and behaviour of different groups of people. Stringer and Molleson measured the skull's size, its thickness, the spacing of its eye sockets, the shape and length of its teeth and other features. The measurements were fed into a computer and compared to data collected from over 2500 different skulls from around the world. Skull shapes and measurements, they knew, vary by race. For example, if the skull was Asian, it would be more rounded than if the skull was European, and its nasal openings closer to the eye sockets. Based on the computer-generated comparisons, Stringer and Molleson concluded that the skull belonged to a girl who was Caucasian.

With this information, police detectives combed the neighbourhood where the body was found, asking questions. Did anyone remember a fair-haired teenager who had lived in the house five to ten years ago? Hundreds of tenants had lived in the house during that period, some for days, others for months. No one could recall a young girl matching that description.

The investigation seemed to have reached a dead end. Without a face, detectives couldn't identify the victim.

Around this time, Sergeant Ron Ashby, a police detective assigned to the case, remembered an article he had read about

Richard Neave, a medical artist at Manchester University who had used modelling clay to create recognizable faces of mummies. He'd done the same with other famous skulls, too — historical figures like Philip II of Macedonia (father of Alexander the Great) and King Midas. Perhaps, Ashby thought, Neave could use the same process to bring the girl's skull to life.

To start, Neave made a copy of the skull from plaster. Next he drilled tiny holes into the copy at twenty-one strategic points — in the forehead, lips, jaw, chin and temple. He inserted wooden pegs of varying length into the holes, each one representing the thickness of flesh. Longer pegs for cheeks and chin; shorter pegs for thin sections like the skullcap.

Neave applied clay to the replica, sculpting the muscle, sinew, cartilage and tendons to give the skin form and texture. Applying the principles of facial anatomy and symmetry, he added the eyes, nose, mouth and ears. Just one day after receiving the skull, Neave had recreated the face of a teenage girl, attractive and on the brink of adulthood.

Police called a news conference. Photos of the reconstructed face were distributed, broadcast on British television and published in newspapers around the country. A poster was made that showed the face. A caption below it read: "Do you know this girl?"

People called with leads, reporting girls who had gone missing. Two of the calls came from social workers who dealt with displaced children. "That's Karen Price," they told police. "She ran away from a children's home."

Police investigated each lead. One by one, they checked off names as the missing girls were accounted for. Within a short time, only one name remained. Karen Price.

From the social workers' files, police obtained a photograph of Price. Using a technique known as skull-face superimposition, a photograph of the skull was placed over the girl's photo. It was a close match. For further proof, Price's dental records were obtained. They were compared to the X-rays taken by Whittaker. These, too, matched closely.

Although the skeleton was almost certainly Karen Price, there was still a small chance that the person in the carpet could have been someone else, perhaps another teenager who closely matched her physical features. To positively identify the victim, forensic experts used another method — DNA fingerprinting.

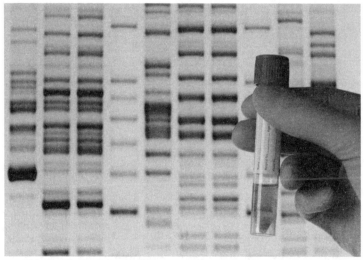

Like conventional fingerprinting, genetic fingerprinting can accurately distinguish humans from one another and can be applied to as little material as a single cell.

A small piece of the skeleton's femur (thigh bone) weighing just 5 grams was sent to Dr. Erika Hagelberg, a leading authority on the process of extracting DNA from ancient bones. To get at the inner structure of the bone where DNA material resided, Hagelberg sandblasted away one or two millimetres of the surface. She divided the bone into two pieces, and extracted 5 micrograms of DNA from each segment. Some of the DNA had deteriorated with time, but a few strands were intact, enough to isolate genetic markers. When these were compared to DNA from Price's parents, there was an unmistakable match to their genetic codes. The odds that the body was someone other than Karen Price were 200,000 to 1.

Scientists had solved the mystery of the skeleton's identity. But who had killed her, and why?

On February 15, 1990, a television crime-watch show profiled Karen Price. She had been a troubled child, under the guardianship of social services for years. She had attended a number of special schools and eventually her family had lost touch with her. Then, after running away from a children's home in July 1981, she had simply vanished.

A viewer who watched the show called with a lead that brought police to Idris Ali, a small-time criminal. After two days of questioning, Ali broke down and told police what had happened. On a summer evening in 1981, in a basement apartment of 29 Fitzhamon Embankment, Ali had witnessed a violent argument between Price and Alan Charlton, a friend of Ali's. Blind with rage, Charlton had beaten Price and, with Ali's help, strangled her. The two had bundled up the body in a carpet and a day later buried it in a backyard grave.

Alan Charlton was arrested. A year later, he was sentenced to life in prison for the murder. Idris Ali, his accomplice, was given a lesser sentence.

With the convictions, the Karen Price story was complete. The skeleton of an unknown girl murdered ten years before had a name, her family had been notified and her killers brought to justice, thanks to the police, media and several kinds of scientists working together.

TOOLS

DNA Fingerprinting

Deoxyribonucleic acid, or DNA, is found in every living cell. It contains a person's genetic blueprint — a code of features that is inherited from both parents. Much of a person's DNA is the same as another's, which is why humans share similar properties, like two eyes, two legs, or one nose. Only 0.2 percent of human DNA is unique to each person. The unique portion gives each human features that make one distinguishable from the other, like having blue eyes instead of brown, being tall rather than short, or having a narrow nose versus wide.

In 1984, Dr. Alec Jeffreys at Britain's University of Leicester developed the method of identifying individual differences in DNA. By isolating unique segments of DNA, attaching radioactive "probes" to them, and then exposing the DNA to X-ray film, Jeffreys was able to produce a DNA image or "fingerprint," similar to a barcode, that was unique for each individual.

Three years later, in a landmark British case, DNA fingerprinting was used for the first time to convict a killer of a double murder. Within a year, it was being used around the world to catch criminals and solve crimes.

The Case of Blackbeard's Missing Queen

The pirate ship was lurking somewhere below the murky water, lost to tides and shifting sands. How could divers ever hope to find it?

One of the most notorious eighteenth-century pirates to make regular runs along America's Atlantic coast was a man of many names. In some circles he was called Edward Teach. History books also refer to him as Edward Thatch, Thache, Tach, Tash and even Drummond. Most people, though, know him better by his nickname — Blackbeard.

In 1717, Blackbeard captured a French slave ship and renamed it *Queen Anne's Revenge*. Roughly 200 tonnes, 30 metres long and carrying forty cannons, the ship was sleek and swift. In time, Blackbeard added three more ships to his fleet, including a Jamaican sloop named *Adventure*.

In mid-May 1718, after a week of plundering ships and holding prisoners for ransom at Charleston, South Carolina, Blackbeard ordered his fleet north. By early June, he had reached the coast of North Carolina. As *Queen Anne's Revenge* swept across an inlet, it struck a sandbar. The crew tried to pull the ship free with a kedge anchor, but failed. When Blackbeard summoned *Adventure* to help, the smaller ship ran aground, too. Both ships were wedged firmly in the sand, and with low tide approaching, Blackbeard ordered his men to abandon the vessels.

A few months later, Blackbeard met a bloody end not too far away. At dawn on November 22, 1718, English ships cornered him at Ocracoke Inlet, North Carolina. Blackbeard fought ferociously, brandishing swords and pistols, but finally fell dead, his body pierced by bullets and stab wounds.

In the early 1700s, Blackbeard plundered ships
all along the eastern coastline of the United States.

By then *Queen Anne's Revenge* and *Adventure* had disappeared below the surface. Pummelled by waves, their hulls smashed by rocks, the ships had filled with water and sunk to the murky bottom, vanishing from view, but not entirely from memory.

In the early 1980s, David Moore, a graduate student in East Carolina University's Maritime History and Nautical Archaeology program, took an interest in locating the wrecks. Fascinated with Blackbeard's story, Moore dug into the pirate's past, intending to write a research paper on the subject.

"Blackbeard had always been seen through the eyes of historians, and I wanted to see him through the eyes of an archaeologist," Moore explained.

Moore started where many good scientists start their research — by determining what was already known. While sifting through the university's archives, he found a 1717 newspaper report of the trial of pirate Stede Bonnet, an accomplice of Blackbeard. The report contained the testimony of Davie Herriot, the original captain of the *Adventure*. Among the details in the report were Herriot's words describing the sinking of Blackbeard's ships: "After they had all got safe into Topsail-Inlet, except Thatch, the said Thatch's ship *Queen Anne's Revenge* run aground off the Bar of Topsail-Inlet . . . "

Moore consulted navigation maps of the 1700s, looking for Topsail Inlet. He found that over the centuries, the name had been changed to Beaufort Inlet. Long ago the entrance to the harbour had been on the westward side of the inlet. Over time, shifting sand had changed its location. One chart published in 1738 showed the position of a sandbar nearby. It also provided sailing directions. By keeping a white house on shore in view, it said, and sailing in a direct line toward it, ships could avoid being beached.

Moore finished his research paper, concluding that *Queen Anne's Revenge* was in Beaufort Inlet. The *Adventure* was, too — somewhere along the sandbar, in sight of a white house on shore.

A few years later while digging through files at the North Carolina Underwater Archaeology Unit (UAU), treasure seeker Phil Masters came across Moore's report. Intrigued, Masters decided to search for Blackbeard's ships. He formed a company called Intersal Inc., found investors to fund the search and received permission from the state to hunt the coast at Beaufort Inlet for the pirate ships.

Masters and his crew criss-crossed the inlet. Using sonar equipment they directed beams of sound into the water. They were hoping for a return echo that would tell them if there were any unusual deposits on the inlet floor. Also towed through the water were magnetometers, sensing devices that detect changes in the strength and direction of magnetic fields. All the while, they followed the clues gathered by Moore, keeping in mind that the white house — still standing — was a key point of reference.

After ten years of searching, Masters and his crew had found little. The murky water held a firm grasp on its secrets. With time running out on the state-issued diving permit, Masters hired a more experienced diver, Mike Daniel. In short order, Daniel located five sites with large debris fields that looked promising.

A widespread debris field was located near the sunken ship.

On November 21, 1996, just two days before the permit was to expire, divers spotted what looked like cannonballs in the sand, a muzzle sticking out from a mound of stone and what appeared to be anchors and cannons caked with deposits from centuries underwater.

The next morning archaeologists from North Carolina UAU arrived on the scene. The sky was grey, the wind on the rise, and the sea choppy. Despite the rough conditions, divers took to the water to see the wreck for themselves. There was no doubt that they had found a ship.

Although little of the hull remained, the size of the debris field, the number of cannons and anchors and the artifacts brought to the surface by Masters's team told them that the vessel had been large and heavily armed. But was it *Queen Anne's Revenge?*

Cannons and cannonballs were brought to the surface by Masters's team.

Marine archaeologists have been working to find proof that the wreck really is *Queen Anne's Revenge*. Without the ship's nameplate, they have to rely on scientific methods.

Magnetometer readings indicate that the wreck is about 30 metres long, a close match to the size of *Queen Anne's Revenge*. Divers have raised over twenty cannons from the site, along with assorted cannonballs and ammunition, indicating that the ship was prepared for heavy combat. Thousands of other artifacts have also been recovered from the wreck. Some are small or broken — shards of glass, musket balls, ceramic fragments. Others are everyday items such as pewter plates with English markings, wine goblets and stoneware storage containers. The range of items, as well as the different countries where they originated, support the idea that this was a pirate ship heavily involved in plunder.

Using other methods of dating artifacts, scientists have determined that the average date of the recovered objects is 1706.

But some of the most useful conclusions come from scientific ways of dating the objects. Divers have brought to the surface samples of wooden timbers as well as other organic (once-living) materials. Organic materials contain carbon, and through a process called radiocarbon dating, scientists can determine the age of carbon-based materials. Radiocarbon dating of timbers from the wreck suggests that the ship was built between 1690 and 1710.

Using other methods of dating artifacts, scientists have determined that the average date of the recovered objects is 1706 — well within the range of Blackbeard's time. Perhaps the single most convincing piece of evidence comes from a recovered bronze bell. When sea growth was removed, a date — *1709* — and the inscription IHS *Maria* appeared. The inscription identified the bell as Spanish in origin. The date indicated that it had been manufactured nine years before the sinking of Blackbeard's ships. While not likely a ship's bell, it was quite possibly one that had been plundered by pirates from a Spanish church or mission.

Today, work on the wreck continues. In May 2011, archaeologists recovered what they believe to be an anchor from *Queen Anne's Revenge*. The ship has been surveyed, mapped, photographed and partially excavated. Confident that they are hot on Blackbeard's trail, marine archaeologists have expanded their search. The *Adventure* is there too, they believe — somewhere below the murky waters, not far away.

The Case of the Embu Skeleton

There was no autopsy and no guests at the funeral. No photographs were taken. Whose body was really in the grave?

Death by drowning was the official cause of death, but from the start there seemed to be more to the story. Wolfgang Gerhard had been swimming in the Atlantic Ocean off the coast of Sao Paulo, Brazil, on February 7, 1979, when he floundered. A friend, Wolfram Bossert, dragged him to shore, but it was already too late. With the help of Bossert's wife, the body was loaded into a car and driven 29 kilometres to the Institute of Forensic Medicine. After a quick examination, a doctor confirmed the death, signed the death certificate and released the body.

Oddly, no autopsy was performed, a normal procedure when death is suspicious or accidental. No photographs were taken of the body, either. Nor did the doctor seem to notice a few discrepancies. The man's ID card stated that Wolfgang Gerhard was fifty-four years old. The man brought in that day appeared to be much older — closer to seventy. He was shorter, too — 173 centimetres tall, not 183 centimetres, as Gerhard was supposed to be.

Shortly after, Gerhard was buried in a cemetery in the Brazilian city of Embu. There was no funeral. There were no invited guests. It was a quiet affair, almost as if no one was supposed to know that he had died. And for six years, hardly anyone did.

The Bosserts eventually disclosed the death in a letter to friends in Germany. The letter tells of the death of their "uncle" and vows to "continue secrecy." In 1985, the letter was discovered by West German police, who notified Brazilian authorities. The possibility that "Uncle" was dead immediately became international news.

"Uncle" was one of the names given to Josef Mengele, a notorious German war criminal. Mengele had been the chief doctor at Auschwitz-Birkenau, a death camp in Poland where at least 1.1 million Jews and almost two hundred thousand other political prisoners were executed during World War II. It was Mengele who had decided the fate of many. He regularly screened new arrivals at the camp, hand-picking some people for cruel and hideous experiments, and deciding which of the others would be sent to the gas chambers. To win the trust of unfortunate victims who had been selected for experimentation, Mengele sometimes introduced himself as Uncle Mengele. To most inmates, though, he was better known as the Angel of Death.

Nazi war criminal Josef Mengele was known as the Angel of Death.

After the war, Mengele lived for a while in Germany under another name. But in 1949, when the hunt for Nazi war criminals intensified, he fled to South America. For the next three decades he lived in obscurity, using false names and moving frequently, always one step ahead of those pursuing him.

With a $3.5 million reward for his capture and several countries involved in the search, the hunt for Mengele was relentless. When word arrived that the body in the Embu grave might be his, there was relief, but also great skepticism. Mengele had been slippery and clever. With the help of allies like the Bosserts, as well as loyal family members in Germany, he had dodged justice for decades. Perhaps this was another trick.

On June 6, 1985, Brazilian police — shovels and machinery ready — met at the cemetery where the body was buried. The grave of Wolfgang Gerhard was hurriedly opened. The remains were removed, but in the rush an overeager worker with a shovel shattered the skull, breaking it into fragments.

The bones were shipped to a laboratory in nearby Sao Paulo. Within a few days, forensic scientists from the United States, Germany and Israel arrived. Armed with specialized equipment and years of expertise, they investigated the remains, hoping to identify the owner. Meanwhile bounty hunters, journalists, television reporters and historians waited to hear the verdict, wondering if a forty-year-old international search might finally be over. Waiting, too, and thirsting for justice were survivors from Auschwitz-Birkenau, many of them subjects of Mengele's cruel experiments.

The bones were inspected by several forensic anthropologists, all top-notch experts in their field. The narrowness of the pelvic bones indicated that the skeleton was a man's. Further measurements of the skull identified the man's race

— Caucasian. From measurements of the femur, the largest leg bone, and the humerus, the long bone of the upper arm, anthropologists calculated the man's height — 173.5 centimetres. By comparing the right humerus and femur with the slightly smaller bones on the left side, they concluded the man must have been right-handed. To determine the man's age, they cut a section of the femur, examined it under the microscope, and counted its blood-carrying canals. Since the number of canals is known to increase with age, they established that the man had been roughly sixty-eight or sixty-nine years old at the time of death.

The results ruled out Wolfgang Gerhard as the body in the grave. The real Wolfgang Gerhard, investigators learned, had once lived in Brazil, but had returned to his native Austria years ago, leaving his identification papers behind. Gerhard had been ten years younger than the body in the grave and considerably taller, too.

But was the body Mengele's?

There were strong similarities between the Embu skull and Mengele's face.

According to German war records, Mengele had been right-handed and 174 centimetres tall during World War II. Born in 1911, he would have been sixty-seven years old in 1979. A photo in Mengele's file showed that he had a high brow, a feature also found on the Embu skull.

Although the skull was damaged, Richard Helmer, a German forensic anthropologist, was able to reassemble the pieces. By overlaying the photo of the skull with a photo of Mengele,

Helmer used video superimposition to determine that there were strong similarities between the Embu skull and Mengele's face. The major features lined up and matched — nose cavity of the skull to the nose of Mengele; eye sockets to the eyes; jaw bones to the position of the mouth. From this test, he determined that it was possible the skull could be Mengele's.

Other evidence proved promising, too. Handwriting experts and document specialists compared samples of Mengele's writing to letters found in the Bosserts' possession. They had been written by the same person, the experts concluded.

After four days of analysis, the team of scientists prepared a report and announced their findings: "It is our opinion that this skeleton is Josef Mengele within a reasonable scientific certainty."

The phrase "within a reasonable scientific certainty" left room for doubt. The likelihood that the skeleton was Mengele's was strong, but in the opinion of the scientists not entirely conclusive. They had uncovered a few troubling discrepancies. In the words of Dr. Clyde Snow, one of the anthropologists, "things just didn't fit the picture."

For one, Mengele had a prominent gap between his front teeth. The Embu skull had no gap. The front teeth were missing and had been replaced by a denture. Wartime records also mentioned that Mengele had suffered from osteomyelitis, an inflammation of the bone marrow, but X-rays of the skeleton showed no trace of the disease.

These discrepancies were resolved shortly after. When dental records for Mengele were finally located, they showed that before dentures there had been a large gap between his front teeth. An expert radiologist who re-examined Mengele's X-rays from Germany that showed he suffered from osteomyelitis questioned the diagnosis. In his opinion, it was quite possible that Mengele never had the disease, but another type of inflammation, one often mistaken for osteomyelitis.

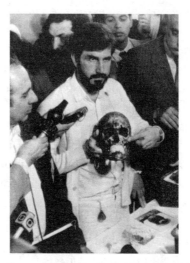

Brazilian anthropologist Daniel Munoz holds up the skull of Nazi war criminal Josef Mengele.

Based on new understandings of the evidence, in 1986 the scientific team revised their report and issued a stronger final statement. "The remains exhumed at Embu Cemetery near Sao Paulo, Brazil, were those of Doctor Josef Mengele," the report read.

But some people involved in the long hunt for Mengele doubted the scientific conclusion. To them, the discovery of the Embu body was just too convenient to be believable. The body was a plant, a close match to Mengele, they maintained. It had been buried in the cemetery by Mengele followers to distract Nazi bounty hunters. The real Mengele was still on the loose, enjoying undeserved freedom.

In 1992, DNA evidence finally settled the matter. DNA

extracted from blood samples obtained from Josef Mengele's son, Rolf, and Irene Hackenjos, his first wife, were compared to DNA secured from the Embu man's femur and humerus. The tests proved with 99.94 percent certainty that Rolf and the man whose skeleton had been found were father and son.

The DNA evidence ended a chase that had lasted decades. The body in the Embu cemetery was the Angel of Death, Josef Mengele.

The Case of the Killer Flu

Young and seemingly fit, the victims drowned in their own bodily fluids. What was causing the mysterious spread of death?

First, a young woman died. She was just twenty-one years old, of Navajo descent and, until illness struck, physically fit and strong. She coached track at the Santa Fe Indian School in New Mexico, jogged, watched what she ate, and led a healthy lifestyle. Then one morning in early May 1993, she woke up to a searing headache, stomach cramps, aches, fever and chills. The flu, she was told by her doctor.

Ten days later, she was gasping for air. Short hours afterwards she collapsed and died. Doctors were mystified. Not knowing the exact cause, they listed the death as the result of adult respiratory distress syndrome.

On May 14, five days after the woman's death, her nineteen-year-old fiancée — also strong and athletic — died on the way to her funeral. Same symptoms — mild flu at first, gasping shortness of breath near the end. Sudden collapse followed by death in a matter of hours.

A medical examination of the two victims showed that their lungs were so soggy with fluid that the organs weighed twice what they should have. Blood had seeped into the puffy lung tissue, filling cavities, making it impossible for the lungs to hold air or transport it to the rest of the body. The victims had quite literally drowned in their own bodily fluids.

Within a week of the woman's death, her brother and his wife developed similar symptoms. Both hovered near death for days. They couldn't seem to breathe either, but they pulled through.

Wary of the widening circle of illness and death, medical examiners combed the Four Corners region, an area bounded by the states of Utah, Colorado, New Mexico and Arizona. Were there others who had suffered the same fate?

They found that five young, seemingly healthy people had died of similar symptoms recently. Clinics were seeing four times as many patients as usual, too. Most were complaining of severe headaches, cramps, nausea, fevers and chills. What was causing the rampant spread of illness?

Dr. James Cheek, a thirty-five-year-old epidemiologist who studied the transmission and control of epidemic diseases with the Indian Health Service, was curious about the strange deaths. Cheek suspected that the victims might have been poisoned by something they had inhaled. To identify the toxin, Cheek visited one of the victim's homes. Most of the belongings had already been moved out and none of the products he found inside seemed to be capable of causing the symptoms he had observed. Even so, Cheek gathered samples of whatever he could find — leftover food, soaps, disinfectants, even rodent droppings found on the floor.

Realizing that poison wasn't the cause and having no other explanation for the spreading illness, Cheek sought help from other experts. Just nine days after the first death, he alerted the Centers for Disease Control and Prevention (CDC) in Atlanta, Georgia, the national agency that handled suspicious outbreaks of disease and infection. *There is something strange going on out here*, Cheek told them. *People are dying. Many of them are Navajo. We can't figure out why.*

The CDC swung into high alert. While one team of scientists studied blood and tissue samples in the CDC laboratory in

Atlanta, another team of specially trained scientists was dispatched to Albuquerque, New Mexico, to investigate the circumstances behind the outbreak.

With samples collected from disease victims, the Atlanta team tried to identify the virus that might be causing the illness, the first step in finding a remedy or cure. After rounds of chemical and biological testing, the results were analyzed and compared to blood and tissue samples from other cases that had been kept on file. There was a match. One type of virus tested positive: hantavirus.

There was disbelief at first. Hantavirus was common in Asia, but it was not a virus researchers expected to see in North America. Furthermore, hantavirus normally infected the kidneys, not the lungs. Was this a new strain?

To identify the exact virus, chief molecular virologist Dr. Stuart Nichol and his CDC team examined its molecular structure and isolated its genetic code. The genetic information proved what scientists feared most. This was a different type of hantavirus, one with unfamiliar properties and no known remedy or means of control. Skeptical and hoping the results might be wrong, scientists ran the tests again and again. It was a new strain of hantavirus, for certain. It was originally called Muerto Canyon virus because of where the outbreak occurred, and later named Sin Nombre (meaning "nameless") virus. The disease caused by the virus was also named — hantavirus pulmonary syndrome or HPS.

While the team in Atlanta isolated and identified the virus, the field team in Albuquerque tried to find out just how and why the virus had spread. They spoke to state health officials and doctors, reviewed patient records, and questioned survivors, their families and members of the Navajo communities that were most affected. What happened? they asked. Have you or your family ever experienced anything like this before?

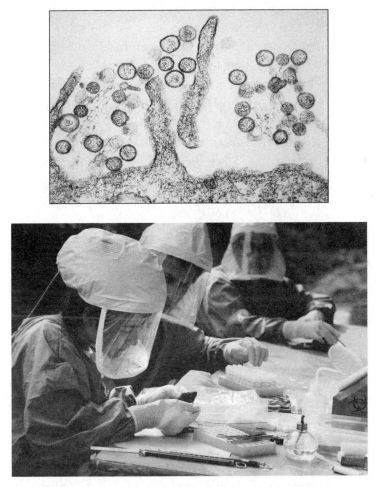

(Upper) A slide from an electron micrograph shows the Sin Nombre hantavirus. (Lower) Three CDC health officials inspect specimens related to a hantavirus outbreak.

When interviewed, Navajo elders launched into a strange story. Three times in the past century there had been epidemics of this type. In each of those years, the weather had been especially wet, and the local piñon trees had produced an abundance of pine nuts. The surplus food attracted mice, rats and other rodents and their numbers had surged. But disease had soon followed — fevers, headaches, gasping for air, death — just like now.

A few things began to make sense. In Asia, the hantavirus was often transmitted to people by rodents like mice and rats. James Cheek had found rodent droppings in one of the victim's houses. The Navajo elders had also mentioned rodents in their story. Was the disease being spread by rodents in the Four Corners area?

A CDC scientist collects specimens from trapped rodents.

To find out, from June to mid-August 1993 almost seventeen hundred rodents were trapped, dissected and tested. Some came from traps set up inside and around the homes of victims, or in places they had been before becoming ill. Others came from traps set up in random locations around the area.

Among the rodents trapped, the deer mouse was found to be

the main host of the hantavirus. In fact, almost thirty percent of the deer mice tested carried the virus. This link between infected rodents and the spread of the disease was strong and convincing.

When investigators compared households where people had gotten the disease to households where people had not, they found an interesting trend. People who became infected had been doing more cleaning around the house or had been working the soil in fields and gardens outside.

Scientists now had a clearer picture of how the virus was being transmitted. It was being passed in the saliva, urine and droppings of infected deer mice, and was living in contaminated dirt and dust. People who worked, played or lived in enclosed places and handled dirt or kicked up infected dust risked breathing in the tiny particles. If they did, the damage to their health was rapid.

Warnings were issued to the public by health organizations to avoid contact with rodents. With precautions in place, spread of the disease waned. Clinics and hospitals reported fewer cases.

One question still lingered, however. Why had the sudden outbreak started in the first place?

An environmental study of the Four Corners region suggested an answer. It echoed the story told by the Navajo elders. Before the outbreak, the Four Corners area had suffered from years of drought. Then in early 1993, heavy snows and rain replenished the region. Plants grew in abundance. With plenty to eat, the deer mouse population boomed.

By May 1993, there were ten times more mice than in May 1992. Chances of human contact increased. So did the chances of transmitting the disease.

While isolating the Sin Nombre virus and halting its spread took scientific skill and teamwork, coincidence might also have been involved. As James Cheek put it later, "I think if it hadn't been for that initial pair of people that became sick within a week of each other, we never would have discovered the illness at all."

IDENTIFIED ━━━━━━━━━━━━━━━━━━━━━

Tracking the Techno Love Bug

One of the most destructive computer viruses ever created was known as The Love Bug. Appearing in e-mail inboxes on May 3, 2000, with the subject line ILOVEYOU, the virus erased files and attached itself to every contact in the computer's address book. Within twenty-four hours, millions of computers in twenty countries around the world were infected. Finding the person responsible for writing the program and distributing the virus became a top-level priority for the Federal Bureau of Investigation (FBI) and other international agencies.

Computer scientists, engineers and other investigators started by dissecting the virus and examining its source code. In the source code, they found the perpetrator's handle (nickname), hometown, the name of a programming group and the word *Barok*. The source code told investigators that the virus had been written by someone named Spyder who lived in the Philippines and belonged to a support group called GRAM-MERSoft.

Using these key words, investigators searched the Internet for more clues. Barok, they found, was the name of another virus that had been posted four months earlier by a student at AMA College in Manila, the capital of the Philippines. A professor at the college recognized the code word *Barok* as being the same one used in a term assignment written by a student named Onel de Guzman. Police searched de Guzman's apartment and discovered disks that proved he had helped create the virus.

Although virus hunters were able to identify the source of the virus and stop its spread, charges against de Guzman eventually had to be dropped. At the time, Philippine laws that prohibited computer hacking were vague, leaving prosecutors without legal grounds to pursue the case.

___

The Case of the Lost Romanovs

"The world will never know what we did with them," one
of the executioners boasted, and for more than seventy
years that was true.

After the Bolshevik Revolution of 1917, Russia's royal family was
exiled to Ekaterinburg. There, 1300 kilometres east of Moscow,
the Romanovs were confined to a few sparsely furnished rooms
on the upper floor of a white stone house, under heavy guard.

On the evening of July 16, 1918, the family had supper
together, said prayers, and then separated. The daughters —
Olga, aged twenty-two; Tatiana, twenty-one; Marie, nineteen;
and Anastasia, seventeen — went to their bedroom. Alexis,
the thirteen-year-old son, went to sleep on a small bed in his
parents' room. Nicholas II, the former emperor, and his wife
Alexandra, the former empress, played cards and then retired
for the evening.

Shortly after midnight, Yakov Yurovsky, a Bolshevik commander, roused the family and their servants. Forty minutes
later, he led the group to a small basement room at the corner of
the house. Men armed with guns crammed into the room and
lined up in two rows. Yurovsky pulled out his revolver and shot
Nicholas point-blank. The others opened fire. In minutes, the
death squad had the job finished — eleven people executed.

The bodies were loaded onto a truck. In the early hours of the
morning, Yurovsky and a few of his men set out down a muddy,
rutted road into the forest north of Ekaterinburg to a spot with
four towering pine trees known as the Four Brothers. Once
rich in coal and peat, the area was now pocked with empty pits
and mines. Here, the bodies were unloaded and tossed down a

narrow mine shaft. To collapse the mine, Yurovsky dropped in several grenades.

When it was over, Yurovsky returned to Ekaterinburg to file a report. The others involved in the assassinations were sworn to secrecy. "The world will never know what we did with them," one boasted. And for almost seventy years that was true.

The rest of the Romanov family had vanished. No one knew their exact fate.

In 1922, after years of revolution and civil war, a new government emerged that united Russia and its surrounding states into one. Called the Union of Soviet Socialist Republics (USSR) or simply the Soviet Union, it was a communist state under strict central leadership. A veil of secrecy and propaganda hid many of the facts surrounding the Romanovs. The public was simply told that, because of his crimes against the people, "Bloody Nicholas" had been executed. The rest of his family had vanished. No one knew their exact fate.

Like most Soviets, filmmaker and crime writer Gely Ryabov accepted the government's version of the story. Then in August 1976, Ryabov visited the house where the Romanovs had been held. While standing at the entrance to the small basement room, Ryabov felt an overwhelming surge of emotion. "I decided that I must get involved with this story," he said. "I felt a moral obligation, a mission that will stay with me until I die." He vowed to find out exactly what had happened to the Romanovs and to make their story public.

An acquaintance introduced Ryabov to Alexander Avdonin, a geologist and amateur historian who had been investigating the Romanovs. Together the men pledged to uncover the truth.

Using his connections, Ryabov gained permission to dig through the Communist party archives in Moscow. From long-hidden letters and reports, Yurovsky's name surfaced. So did details of the execution. The bodies had been dumped in a mine shaft outside of Ekaterinburg, Ryabov learned. Soon after the burial, word of the location had leaked out. Determined to keep the site a secret, Yurovsky had returned the next day, removed the bodies, ordered soldiers to smash the faces of the victims to make them unrecognizable, and then tossed the remains into a newly dug hole in the middle of the road. Sulfuric acid was poured over the bodies to dissolve them. Dirt was thrown on top, followed by a layer of railway ties. There was no mention, though, of the grave's exact location.

Ryabov tracked down Yurovsky's eldest son. He was a retired admiral living in Moscow who was willing to share what he knew. The man reached into a desk drawer and pulled out four yellowed sheets. "When my father died," he told Ryabov, "he left this in his papers."

On the pages, in Yurovsky's own words, was his secret report to the Communist party Central Committee. The details Ryabov had uncovered earlier were all there, but there was new information, too. When Yurovsky and his men returned the day after the execution, they had reburied the remains in two graves, not one. The bodies of Alexis and one of his sisters were burned in a bonfire. The charred remains — ash and bits of bone — were shovelled into the ground. The other bodies went into a common grave, a pit 1.8 metres deep and 2.5 metres square.

Yurovsky's report pinpointed the exact location of the secret grave — 19 kilometres northwest of Ekaterinburg, at a spot where railroad tracks crossed a winding dirt road.

Using the clues Ryabov had uncovered, Avdonin began a search of the region around Ekaterinburg with the help of another geologist. In the sixty years since the executions, much of the landscape had changed. The old road was gone, replaced now by swamp and grass. But the geologists knew that the surface of a landscape often hints at what might be underneath. Hollows or depressions in the ground could mean that the soil had settled over an opening or pit. Mounds, hills and ridges could indicate that roads, foundations or walls were below.

For a better look, one of the geologists climbed a tree. From his perch, he spotted a pattern of parallel ridge marks in the ground. "I see where the railway ties are buried," he cried.

The two men constructed a simple instrument — a sharpened steel water pipe that resembled a large corkscrew. Using the device, they walked along the path of ridges, every now and then pounding the instrument into the ground.

"We hit something soft like wood at a depth of forty centimetres," Avdonin said. "We moved here and there, drilling all around, and discovered an area approximately 2 metres by 3 metres where there was evidence of wood beneath the surface."

Was this the burial site? Knowing that they were probing into a well-kept government secret, the men were afraid of being discovered. In the Soviet Union, people were often jailed without trial for lesser reasons. Fearful of being caught, the men left, vowing to keep the information hidden.

Three years later, Ryabov and Avdonin returned to the site. Using Avdonin's core sampler, they bored deep into the soil to take samples of the layers of dirt underneath. In some samples, the layers were scrambled and mixed together, indicating that at one time the earth below had been disturbed. Streaks of black, oily clay ran along the bottom. The soil emitted a foul, acid-like smell, a clear indication that strong chemicals were present.

Certain that this was the gravesite, they dug straight down. They found the railway ties, and directly below, a bluish-black bone and three skulls. One was clearly an adult's. The second was slightly smaller and oval-shaped — a young woman's. There was a small hole on one side of the skull and a much larger hole opposite it: entrance and exit holes from a bullet, it seemed. The third skull was smaller still — a child's, perhaps. It was difficult to say. The facial bones of the three skulls were either damaged or missing entirely.

Anxious to leave, they bundled up the skulls, covered their tracks and drove back to town. There the men divided up the skulls. Avdonin took the largest one and hid it under his bed. Ryabov took the other two back to Moscow and kept them in his apartment.

Yet the fear of being caught was too much. The men returned to the gravesite a year later to rebury the three skulls. As they dug into the soft soil, another skull surfaced. It was as if the dead were calling out. But it was too dangerous to continue. The skulls were returned to the ground, the site covered and disguised, hidden once more.

Nine years passed. Gradually, the Soviet Union underwent sweeping changes. Feeling that it was finally safe to reveal the secret, Ryabov published a magazine article about the discovery. The news circulated around the globe, stirring interest. Avdonin requested permission to reopen the grave and received government approval.

In July 1991, the earth was carefully removed and sifted for evidence. The three skulls Avdonin and Ryabov had discovered earlier were found. Digging deeper, searchers located more skulls, hundreds of bone fragments and fourteen bullets.

In the foreground are the skulls of the deposed Czar Nicholas (right) and Czarina Alexandra Feodorovna (left).

Forensic anthropologists sorted the bones into groups based upon size, shape and other features. There were nine skeletons, they decided. Five female. Four male. Five of the individuals seemed to have common traits and were thought to be from the same family. One of the skulls had expensive porcelain crowns, a match to the type of dental work Empress Alexandra once had done.

In July 1992, nine femur bones — one from the thigh of each individual — were sent to England for DNA testing. To establish family relationships, DNA was extracted from each femur and compared to the other eight. Five matched — two adults and three children. Next, DNA from the five was compared to DNA taken from locks of hair from the royal family that been stored in a Russian museum. Again there was a match. Finally, the DNA was compared to DNA extracted from hair and blood samples donated by living descendants of both Nicholas and Alexandra. One of these donors was England's Prince Philip, the Duke of Edinburgh, a blood relative of Nicholas II.

On July 9, 1993, the British forensic team announced its findings. The DNA tests provided convincing evidence, confirming what Avdonin and Ryabov had long suspected. Almost certainly, these were the bones of Nicholas, Alexandra and three of their daughters — Olga, Tatiana and Anastasia.

In 1998, on the eightieth anniversary of their murders, the five members of the Romanov family were reburied in the royal crypt of St. Peter and Paul Cathedral in St. Petersburg. The ceremony was attended by relatives of the Romanovs as well as dignitaries and officials of the Russian government.

A chapter seemed closed; the dead finally at rest. But there was still one mystery left to solve. Nine skeletons had been found in the burial pit, but there had been eleven victims. Where were the others?

As it turned out, Alexis and Marie were not far away. In 2007, Sergei Plotnikov, a forty-six-year-old builder and part of a team of amateur archaeologists who spent weekends searching for the graves of the two missing Romanov children, discovered something unusual as he searched the field just 60 metres from the main burial site. As Plotnikov probed the soil, he hit something hard. "There was a crunching sound," he said. "This means you've hit coal or bone."

Plotnikov called other members of the search team over. "We found several bone fragments. The first was a piece of pelvis. We then discovered a fragment of skull. It had clearly come from a child."

More than forty bone fragments ranging in size from a few millimetres to several centimetres, as well as seven teeth, three bullets and part of a dress, were unearthed. The bones were charred and damaged. "It was clear they didn't die peacefully," Plotnikov said.

DNA tests on the bone fragments confirmed what archeologists suspected. These were the two missing Romanov children — Alexis and Marie.

With this discovery, the mystery of the Romanovs seemed to be solved, but even so, the case is still immersed in controversy. The Russian Orthodox Church refuses to acknowledge that the remains are those of the Romanovs, claiming that the initial investigation was shoddy, and that the conclusions are questionable.

Scientists also differ in their opinions. Some argue that because DNA erodes with time, the DNA tests conducted in 1992 are far from reliable evidence. Since then, methods of DNA extraction and testing have improved, and critics say that the previous DNA tests should be repeated to substantiate the conclusion.

Meanwhile scientists who worked on the original analysis stand by their results. To them, the bones are without a doubt those of the Romanovs, and the final chapter of their story is closed.

TOOLS

Disappearing DNA

Over time, DNA in tissue and bone deteriorates. The double-helix strands of the molecule become damaged and the DNA breaks into very small fragments. If the fragments are too damaged, too small, or are contaminated with other genetic material, DNA testing might be impossible.

Temperature, humidity and acidity can speed up or slow down the deterioration rate. A mummy thousands of years old can be an excellent source of DNA if its tissues are well preserved. On the other hand, a more recently buried body might be a poor source if the surrounding soil was highly acidic or if the body was subjected to wet and warm conditions that accelerated decay.

Scientists Find the Answers

- *Gone south for the winter, but where?*
  Until 1975, the winter home of the eastern monarch butterfly was a mystery. To track its location, Canadian entomologists Fred and Norah Urquhart and a team of supporters fixed tiny tags to the wings of thousands of monarchs and then charted their locations as they were retrieved on their journey south. After decades of dedicated research, the Urquharts finally identified the location of the monarchs' winter home — the "Mountain of Butterflies" near Angangueo, Mexico.

- *Where did signals from outer space come from?*

In 1967, while searching for distant signals with a radio telescope, astronomers Jocelyn Bell-Burnell and Antony Hewish detected something unexpected — regular pulses coming from several locations beyond the solar system, but still within the Milky Way galaxy. A number of explanations were considered, from radar being reflected off the moon to the possibility that "little green men" in outer space might have sent the signals. After discounting each explanation, only one possibility remained. The signals had to be coming from a new type of star. Eventually, the team identified the source — compact stars known as pulsars or "neutron stars." The discovery of pulsars opened up a whole new branch of astrophysics and earned Hewish a Nobel Prize for Physics.

- *What do the ancient squiggles really mean?*

Over a hundred and fifty years ago, a circular clay tablet was unearthed at Nineveh, the capital of what was once Assyria, in the Middle East. Scratched into the surface of the tablet were drawings of constellations as well as indecipherable picture-messages. Scientists were unable to interpret the tablet until 2008 when two aeronautics engineers, Alan Bond and Mark Hempsel, cracked the code using a computer program that showed what the night sky looked like thousands of years ago. By comparing the star pattern on the tablet to images generated by the computer, they were able to identify the tablet as an ancient notebook used by astronomers over five thousand years ago. Etched into the tablet was a match to the stars and constellations that existed on the night of June 29, 3123 B.C.

CHAPTER 2
PROVE

Introduction

The phone call was a strange one, and it took Dr. Stephen O'Brien by surprise. O'Brien was the head of Animal Genetics at the Laboratory of Genomic Diversity in Frederick, Maryland. On the line was Roger Savoie, a Royal Canadian Mounted Police (RCMP) investigator. There had been a murder. The RCMP had a suspect, but no witnesses and not much evidence — just a few stray cat hairs. Could O'Brien and his team of genetic scientists extract cat DNA from them? Dr. O'Brien was intrigued.

The case involved a missing woman — Shirley Duguay, a thirty-two-year-old mother of five. In May 1995, seven months after her disappearance, the RCMP found Duguay's badly decomposed body in a shallow grave near the small town of North Enmore, Prince Edward Island. Not far away was a plastic bag containing a man's blood-soaked leather jacket. Tests showed that the blood on the jacket belonged to Duguay.

The suspect was Duguay's recently paroled ex-husband, Douglas Beamish, a man with a quick temper and a history of violence. What little evidence there was didn't link Beamish directly to the crime.

On the jacket, however, forensic investigators had found

44

unusual white hairs. Tests showed that the hairs had come from a cat. One of the RCMP officers recalled that Beamish's parents owned a white cat named Snowball. If the DNA from the hair matched Snowball's DNA, perhaps police could connect Beamish to the murder.

Using a method developed by scientists at the Maryland laboratory, DNA from the root of one of the hairs was obtained. A sample of Snowball's blood was drawn. When the DNA from the hair was compared to DNA from Snowball's blood, they were the same. To rule out that the hair might belong to a close relative of Snowball and to prove that the testing method was valid, twenty other cats on P.E.I. were also tested. None of their DNA matched the hair's except Snowball's.

At the trial, the jury heard about Beamish's violent past, the threats he had uttered against his wife, and how he had been seen wearing a leather jacket similar to the one found near the grave. The most compelling proof, though, came from Snowball, since the cat's hair linked Beamish directly to the body.

In 1996, Beamish was convicted of second-degree murder and sentenced to life in prison. The case made forensic history. It was the first time an animal's DNA was used to connect a murder suspect to a victim.

The cases in this chapter follow a similar thread. Scientists are asked to establish proof, to decide based on evidence who is guilty or what is to blame. As with Snowball's hair, the proof is not always obvious. Concealed in the grit of an oily smear, in shards of twisted metal, or in chemicals embedded in paper, the evidence might be hidden, waiting for scientists to discover it.

The Case of *Columbia's* Final Flight

Bits of the shuttle landed in yards, swimming pools and open fields from East Texas to Louisiana. What caused Columbia *to disintegrate?*

On the morning of February 1, 2003, *Columbia* re-entered Earth's atmosphere travelling at 27,000 kilometres per hour. Pulled by gravity, the space shuttle slammed into air molecules, creating friction that superheated its surface. Disintegration of the spacecraft began moments later. As the shuttle streaked over Utah, Nevada and Arizona, chunks of it started to spiral away. Around the same time, sensors on *Columbia's* left side signalled warnings to Mission Control, first along the wing, then in the left landing gear.

As *Columbia* tore over Texas, it rolled and pitched, flew backwards for a time, recovered, then somersaulted out of control. The left wing separated. The tail, right wing and main body followed. Last to go was the crew cabin. It hovered for a second before breaking into fragments.

The air crackled and boomed, rumbling so loudly that some people below dropped to the ground in fear. Thousands of pieces of debris fell from the sky, cutting a swath 16 kilometres wide by 480 kilometres long that stretched from Texas to Louisiana. Some chunks were pebble-sized — nuts, bolts, scraps of heat tiles, bite-sized pieces of the control panel. Others were massive, the size of small cars and weighing hundreds of kilograms — wing sections, engine parts, shredded fuel compartments.

Bits of *Columbia* landed in yards and fields, streams and swamps. One ripped a hole in a backyard trampoline. Another small piece hit the window of a moving car. Luckily, no one on the ground was killed or injured. The crew was not as fortunate. All seven astronauts on board the shuttle were killed.

News of the tragedy spread worldwide, stirring grief and raising questions. In the long history of *Columbia* there had been 111 successful re-entries, each one precise and nearly flawless. *Columbia* was a tried-and-true workhorse, a remarkable flying machine. How could such a thing happen?

From the start, staff at National Aeronautics and Space Administration (NASA) had a suspect, a possible source of *Columbia*'s fatal problem. Eighty-two seconds after liftoff, a piece of foam insulation the size of a small suitcase and weighing less than a kilogram had broken away from the external fuel tank and smashed into the shuttle's left wing. Video footage of the launch had captured the moment, and early into the mission NASA managers had analyzed the tape, discussed its implications and argued about what to do. They decided in the end not to do anything. The foam strike, NASA figured, had inflicted only minor damage, nothing that would hinder the mission or endanger the crew.

But now there were doubts about that decision. Had the foam strike been the cause of the disaster? Could NASA's assessment of the damage have been wrong?

Within hours an investigation into the *Columbia* disaster was launched. Over the next days and weeks, phones at NASA rang as Texans located parts of the spacecraft. Search teams followed up on leads, scoured the countryside, gathered mangled pieces and charted the location of every scrap, no matter how small or seemingly insignificant. The more data the team of investigators could gather, the better their chances of finding answers.

More than eighty-four thousand pieces of *Columbia* were

recovered. The bulk of the debris was located under the main break-up area, but some pieces were found in far-flung places. There were also a number of surprises, like a vacuum cleaner that landed intact, still in working order, and worms from an on board science experiment that survived. The shuttle's nose cap was discovered crushed and pasted into the soil.

Identified main fuselage debris is laid out on the grid system in the hangar.

Some discoveries were more significant than others. Near Hemphill, Texas, a firefighter walking over hilly terrain spotted a square metal box lying flat on the ground. Hardly scratched, it was the modular auxiliary data system recorder from *Columbia*, one of the objects most essential to the investigation. The track tape contained the flight data — computer records of the space shuttle's last moments.

One of the more eerie finds was made near Palestine, Texas. Searchers had almost finished their rounds when they noticed a small rectangular plastic object. It was a videotape shot by astronaut Laurel Clark recording some of the final moments on *Columbia*'s flight deck — smiling faces, excited voices, space travellers unaware of what was to come.

A reconstruction team member matches puzzle pieces of debris material.

The wreckage was hauled to a hangar at the Kennedy Space Center in Florida, tagged and laid across a grid along the floor. Gradually a skeleton-like outline of *Columbia*'s exterior began to take shape. Engineers and flight specialists analyzed the debris, looking for answers in the twisted and burnt pieces. There were gaps and holes, places where wreckage was missing or where pieces were barely recognizable. The most severe damage was to the left wing. Whatever had started *Columbia* on its death spiral had originated there. The finger of blame pointed to liftoff, to the moment of impact by the fly-away foam.

At the same time, other investigators reviewed the computer data collected by Mission Control during re-entry, noting again the sensor warnings issued just before *Columbia* tore apart. The data found on the shuttle's modular auxiliary data system recorder were studied, too. Hundreds of bits of information were still intact, each one adding clues. Like the debris, they pointed to the same cause. There had been problems during re-entry, losses of pressure and increased heat on the left side. Once again damage in the shuttle's left wing by the foam seemed to be the reason.

Before a final judgment could be issued, independent impact tests were ordered. These were conducted by Southwest Research Institute in San Antonio, Texas. Using a compressed-air gun with an 11-metre barrel, chunks of foam the same size, shape and weight as the original were fired at the same estimated speed at mock-up panels of the shuttle's wing.

Most of the chunks ricocheted off the panels, causing little damage. Angles were changed, firings retried, more targets pummelled. On the last round of attempts, foam was shot from the gun at 800 kilometres per hour, hitting the panel at a 25-degree angle. When the dust cleared, an audible gasp travelled the room. There was a ragged 40-centimetre hole in the panel, larger than a ten-pin bowling ball.

The crew of the ill-fated *Columbia* mission.

The impact test confirmed what many suspected and some at NASA feared. The foam unleashed at liftoff, the same foam NASA managers had discounted as insignificant, could have damaged the left wing's thermal protection system, leaving the shuttle exposed to the forces and heat of re-entry, and causing the break-up.

In its report, investigators chided NASA, citing the agency as being part of the problem. By minimizing the hazards of the foam strike, NASA had failed to act, and in doing so had put the mission in danger.

PROVEN

Collapse at the Hyatt Regency

On a summer night in 1981, hundreds of people were watching a dance contest in the atrium of the Hyatt Regency Hotel in Kansas City, Missouri, when the second- and fourth-floor walkways collapsed without warning. The toll was devastating: 114 dead and over 200 injured, many critically.

Immediately an investigation was launched. The Hyatt was combed for evidence. Photographs were snapped, measurements taken, samples of debris collected. The walkways' crossbeams and hanger rods were inspected for flaws and weaknesses. Structural engineers conducted stress tests on steel components in the lab. The hanger rods connecting the walkways were stretched until they snapped so that the maximum forces the rods supported could be measured. The load capability of beams from the site was compared to those of newly made duplicates to verify the integrity of the metal. At the same time, architects, engineers and contractors were questioned, and plans for the building were scrutinized.

The investigation revealed that during construction a fatal change had been made to the design plans. Originally, the plans called for the second-floor walkway to hang below the fourth-floor walkway by *continuous* steel rods threaded through the crossbeams of each walkway. In this design, the walkways would support their weight independently.

In the new design, to save time and money, *separate* hanger rods had been used. One set of rods led from the roof through holes in the crossbeams of the fourth-floor walkway. A second, separate set of rods led from other holes in the fourth-floor crossbeams to the second-floor walkway underneath. In this plan, there were twice as many holes in the fourth-floor crossbeams as in the original, making the crossbeams weaker. Furthermore, the crossbeams — not the ceiling hangers — now bore the weight of both walkways.

The investigators found that the design change was a recipe for disaster. On the night of the collapse, with both walkways crowded, the fourth-floor crossbeams bore double the load. The metal around the holes in the welded joints split, starting the walkway on a downward plunge that took the second-floor walkway, and many lives, with it.

The Case of the Oily Smear

The murder was a cold-hearted act. Police had few leads and even less evidence.

At about eight in the morning on February 3, 1982, eight-year-old Rajesh Gupta left his home in Scarborough, Ontario. Wearing a hooded ski jacket, a red and white tuque and an orange scarf, the boy trudged through the freshly fallen snow to school. It was a ten-minute walk, following a route Rajesh had taken many times before.

Rajesh never made it to school. Hours later, his body was found face down in the snow on a dead-end street in the north end of the city. At first glance, it seemed the boy might have been the victim of a hit-and-run accident. A smear of dirty oil ran along the back of his jacket, which could have come from the undercarriage of a car.

But when police took a closer look at the body, the awful truth was revealed. Deep indentations ringed his neck, marking places where the cords from his hood had been used to strangle him. Rajesh had been murdered.

The boy's death raised a flood of outrage. The murder was a callous act, committed against a defenseless small boy. His body had been left lying on the side of the road. Sergeant Gord Wilson, the Toronto homicide detective who headed the investigation, described it as, "the way you'd toss a coffee cup from a car."

At the beginning, police had few leads or suspects. Then, as they interviewed family members and gathered information provided by the public, a name emerged — Sarabjit Kaur Minhas, a woman who had been engaged to Rajesh's uncle, Vijay Gupta. The relationship between the two had soured, and although there had been plans to wed, those plans were quashed when Vijay married another woman. Minhas had not taken the news well. She vowed to even the score, to punish Vijay for leaving her, and she had haunted the family with threats and disturbing phone calls.

But suspicion and proof are two different things. To bring the case to court, police had to establish an undeniable link between Minhas and the boy's murder. That link, they believed, might be in the dirt and grime — the oily smear — that ran along the back of Rajesh's jacket.

William Graves, a forensic geologist with the Centre of Forensic Sciences in Toronto, was called. Samples of the oily material were collected from the boy's clothes. Samples were also collected from the floors of eleven indoor parking garages in the area, including one where Minhas parked her Honda automobile.

Graves strained each sample to remove fine particles like sand and glass. Then he analyzed the remaining liquid for thickness, consistency and composition. Using microscopes, he checked the sieved particles for size, shape and colour. Instruments known as spectroscopes were used to analyze the chemical composition of the samples.

In the oily sample drawn from the boy's clothes, Graves found various grades of sand and three types of glass: tempered glass like that used for car windows; thin glass, the kind used in light bulbs; and amber glass of the type used in beer bottles. He also discovered particles of yellow paint with small beads of glass having highly reflective qualities attached to them. The paint was unique, the kind often used to mark centre stripes on highways.

Graves compared these substances to those found in the samples drawn from garages in the area. Most differed in significant ways: the oil was a different brand or grade; the percentage of sand was higher or lower; the particles were larger or smaller; the fragments of paint and glass were thicker, thinner or missing entirely. Only one sample was a close match — the one drawn from Minhas's garage.

Refractive tests were run on the glass fragments in the samples. Light was shone through the glass, the degree of refraction (bending) was measured, and calculations were performed to establish the refractive index of each sample. The numbers, as distinctive as fingerprints in some ways, were unique for each type of glass.

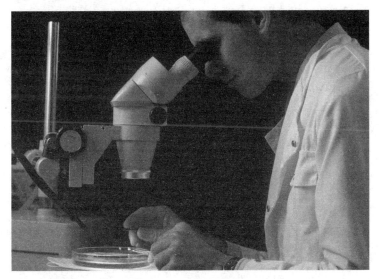

A scientist uses a microscope to analyze small pieces of evidence.

When Minhas's Honda was examined, tiny bits of glass were found inside. Refractive tests showed that they were identical to those found on the boy's clothing. Further investigation revealed that at one point, a beer bottle had smashed the rear window of the Honda, spraying fine glass particles inside the vehicle and on the garage floor.

Police now had a clearer picture of the events leading to the boy's death. On his way to school, Rajesh had likely been offered a lift by Minhas. She had been a trusted friend — his uncle's fiancée — and he had probably accepted the ride, not realizing the danger. Scorned and vengeful, Minhas had strangled the boy in the car or perhaps in the garage, and had inadvertently smeared his jacket with gritty oil. Then she had driven the body to a remote area of town and dumped it by the side of the road.

No one had seen her commit the crime, and Minhas believed her deed would never be discovered. Little did she know that microscopic pieces of glass, paint and sand would point the blame directly at her.

In November 1983, Sarabjit Minhas was tried for murder. One of the witnesses called to testify was forensic geologist William Graves. Using facts and figures and the evidence gleaned from his investigation, Graves provided the jury with a convincing link between the accused and the crime.

Minhas was convicted of first-degree murder and sentenced to life in prison with no chance of parole for twenty-five years.

The Case of the Nervous Traveller

To the U.S. Customs inspector, the driver of the green Chrysler seemed nervous and jittery. What exactly was he hiding?

Night had just fallen one December day in 1999 when a dark green Chrysler sedan rolled off the ferry that shuttled passengers between Victoria, British Columbia, and Port Angeles, Washington. The driver was a thirty-two-year-old man, slim and slightly built, with hazel eyes and dark hair. To U.S. Customs inspector Diana Dean, he seemed nervous and jittery. "Hinky," she would later describe it.

When Dean asked the man the usual questions — Where are you from? Where are you going? For what reason? — he shuffled in his seat. Although he answered in English, he had an accent that was hard to identify. His answers were brisk, one or two words at best. He was from Montreal, he said. He was heading to Seattle for a visit. The man fumbled through the car's console looking for papers. Rather than showing his passport or driver's licence, he pulled out a Costco card.

Dean sensed that something wasn't right. She asked the man to turn off his car, open the trunk and step aside. By this time, other customs workers had finished their own inspections and came to help. The ferry was the last of the day, the Chrysler the final car, and afterwards they could all go home.

Dean used a code word to describe her suspicions. The car might be a "load" vehicle, she hinted. To her fellow inspectors, the word meant one thing. The man might be trying to smuggle something over the border, probably drugs.

The trunk was searched. Inspectors found a suitcase and,

inside the spare-tire compartment, four small black plastic boxes, two pill bottles, two jars of thick brown liquid, and green plastic garbage bags containing fine white powder.

The driver was patted down for weapons. When one of the inspectors pulled off the man's coat to examine it, he fled. Inspectors chased him down the street and through busy intersections. A few blocks away, they cornered the man and turned him over to police. While the search of the trunk continued, the man waited in a nearby patrol car, under guard and carefully watched.

The white powder tested negative for heroin, speed and cocaine. If the powder wasn't a drug, then what was it?

The brown liquid was especially curious. When one of the inspectors held up a jar and shook it, police couldn't help but notice the man's reaction: he ducked and cowered in the patrol car, more nervous than ever.

Within a day or two, the inspectors understood why. The contents of the trunk contained bomb components. The white powder was identified as urea, a chemical used in fertilizers and explosives. The black boxes were homemade timing devices made of circuit boards, nine-volt batteries and inexpensive watches. The brown liquid was a highly unstable explosive, similar to nitroglycerin, but twice as powerful as TNT. Even a slight jiggle of the jars might be enough to trigger a chemical reaction.

The man's passport identified him as Benni Antoine Noris, a resident of Montreal, but even that was suspicious. As well as English, the man spoke French, but not with the usual accent of someone from Montreal. His French sounded foreign.

Algerian Ahmed Ressam carried a false Canadian passport when he attempted to enter the United States.

The FBI was called. FBI inspectors contacted the Canadian Security Intelligence Service (CSIS) and the RCMP. Canadian records showed that the man's name was really Ahmed Ressam, an Algerian with strong connections to Islamic terrorists. What started as a drug bust now seemed more sinister — a terrorist plot to bomb an unknown location in the United States.

U.S. intelligence had been on high alert for such a possibility. Rumours had been flying for weeks that Islamic terrorists were planning a full-scale attack on a number of key sites across the country. Timed to coincide with New Year's Eve festivities that celebrated the new millennium, an attack like this would inflict massive damage. With people in a festive mood, crowded together in tight spaces with their guard down, the body count would undoubtedly be high. Was Ahmed Ressam part of this larger terrorist plot?

To prove that he was a terrorist, investigators needed to show that Ressam not only purchased and handled the bomb components, but that he also knew how to use them and fully intended to target a site in the United States.

Investigators from both the FBI and RCMP dug into Ressam's past, retracing his steps, checking his travel patterns and following links to his friends and family. Ressam had been living in Montreal for several years, they found, but had returned to Algeria a number of times. At least once he had travelled to Afghanistan, where fledgling terrorists sometimes went for training by al-Qaeda. Ressam had a network of friends in Canada, some of whom were known to police — a few for their al-Qaeda connections. They met frequently, often in secret locations.

On November 17, 1999, a few weeks before the ferry ride that brought Ressam to Port Angeles, investigators determined that he and a friend had flown to Vancouver. The two had rented a cottage on the outskirts of the city. They paid cash in advance for two weeks. They also rented a car — the dark green Chrysler. The men kept to themselves, making frequent trips to nearby stores and rarely requesting housekeeping or other services. The cottage window was often left open. Staff commented on the noxious, cologne-like smell that frequently wafted from the room.

Forensic scientists from the FBI and RCMP searched the Vancouver cottage and Ressam's apartment in Montreal. The rooms were combed for fingerprints and stray hairs. Clothes, shoes, books, receipts, packing tape, tools — things worn or possibly used by Ressam — were photographed, catalogued and placed in plastic bags. In a laboratory, these items were examined for fibres, fingerprints, skin cells and other trace evidence that might connect them to the explosive devices found in the rented car.

In the Montreal apartment, investigators found a pair of wool pants and black suede shoes. DNA extracted from skin residue on the items matched Ressam's, proving that the articles were his. Both items had burn holes, likely caused by splashes of acid, an ingredient used to make explosives. When Ressam's legs were examined, a large burn was discovered on his skin that was consistent in size, position and composition to the ones in the pants and shoes.

A datebook covered with thirteen of Ressam's fingerprints contained addresses of known terrorist collaborators.

Investigators also found an illegal 9-mm handgun in the apartment, wrapped in a shirt and hidden inside a stove. A datebook covered with thirteen of Ressam's fingerprints contained addresses of known terrorist collaborators. It also had names and addresses of firms that had sold electronic supplies and chemicals identical to those used in the bomb-making devices found in the car.

More connections to Ressam were found inside the black boxes. Wire insulation matched bits of insulation recovered from the Vancouver cottage. Clear tape used to fasten components in the timing devices matched the chemical composition of a roll of tape found in the Montreal apartment. A hair was discovered on the tape inside one of the boxes. Compared under a microscope to one of Ressam's hairs, it had the same shape, structure, thickness and pigmentation. Fingerprints found on the black boxes were identified as his as well.

Most disturbing of the evidence collected was a folded map

of Los Angeles in the Montreal apartment. Circles had been drawn around three of the area's airports. One was the Los Angeles International Airport, the fifth busiest in the world and Ressam's likely target. On New Year's Eve, it would be filled with travellers. A suitcase packed with explosives and left in a key location would have gone unnoticed. Detonated by timing devices, the bomb would have caused massive damage.

Ressam was charged with nine counts of criminal activity ranging from smuggling and the transportation of explosives to planning an act of terrorism. During a nineteen-day trial, almost 120 witnesses were called to testify in front of a jury. Some of these were forensic experts who, in clear and certain terms, presented the facts uncovered by science.

On April 6, 2001, the jury issued their verdict: Ressam was guilty of all charges. Facing up to 130 years in prison, Ressam co-operated with the U.S. and other governments, releasing important information about al-Qaeda's organization and its terrorist plans. He also confirmed the foiled 2000 millennium plot to bomb the Los Angeles International Airport and other busy U.S. locations.

For his cooperation, Ressam received a lighter sentence. In July 27, 2005, he was sentenced to twenty-two years in prison. In February 2010, that decision was overturned. The court judged the sentence to be unfair and too lenient, and ordered that a more severe punishment be considered.

The Case of the Hitler Diaries

To some, the diaries were a great find; to others, a suspicious discovery. What proof did the publisher have that the diaries were authentic?

On April 25, 1983, the West German magazine *Stern* announced a shocking discovery. Secret diaries handwritten by Adolf Hitler had been found — a total of sixty-two volumes. The magazine promised to publish the diaries, word for word, in future editions. It also agreed to sell the rights to other newspapers and magazines around the world who wanted to do the same.

Immediately, word of the find spread around the globe, sparking discussion and debate. To optimists, the diaries were one of the greatest historical treasures of the century. Here was the opportunity of a lifetime, the chance to delve into the mind of the Nazi leader and discover his version of events during World War II. But skeptics found it hard to believe. How did *Stern* stumble upon the diaries? they wanted to know. What proof did the publisher have that they were authentic?

A page from what was said to be Hitler's diary.

In the face of such scrutiny, an intriguing story surfaced, bringing with it a puzzle and even more questions.

In 1979, Gerd Heidemann, a *Stern* reporter, had visited an acquaintance who collected Nazi memorabilia. On the shelf of a display case in the man's home, Heidemann spotted a thin black book. Two red eagles, symbols of Nazi power, were stamped on the cover. The pages inside were yellow with age and covered in stiff handwriting. It was Hitler's diary, the man told Heidemann. There were at least five other volumes in existence. Maybe more.

Immediately, Heidemann recognized the opportunity. No doubt *Stern* would be interested in the diaries and willing to pay handsomely to publish them. But Heidemann knew that before *Stern* would dish out a penny, the publisher would want proof that the diaries were really Hitler's. Was there some way of verifying them? There was, his acquaintance told him. The diaries had a history that seemed remarkable, but true.

According to the man's story, in 1945, when it seemed that Germany was about to lose the war, the diaries were smuggled out of Berlin aboard a Nazi plane. To protect them from damage, they were locked inside a metal-lined container. En route, the plane had crashed and burned near the village of Boernersdorf, Germany. Farmers had rushed to help; they retrieved the diaries and stored them in a secret location.

Heidemann investigated the story. He travelled to Boernersdorf, talked to villagers, dug through the town's archives and discovered a thin line of truth. In April 1945, a German plane had crashed and burned near Boernersdorf. According to local residents, it had been carrying a mysterious cargo — a container filled with at least twenty-seven diaries. The diaries had been smuggled out of the country by a high-ranking German officer. Now a man named Konrad Fischer, who lived in Stuttgart, Germany, had the others.

Based on this information, Heidemann approached the publishers of *Stern*. To his delight, they offered 2 million German marks ($850,000 U.S. at the time) in exchange for the twenty-seven volumes. Through his acquaintance, Heidemann tracked down Fischer and struck a deal. Heidemann would pay Fischer for the diaries with the money provided by *Stern*. In return, Fischer would give him the diaries.

Fischer imposed a few conditions, small ones, nothing that seemed too out of the ordinary. For one, Heidemann had to promise to keep his source a secret. At no time could he reveal Fischer's name to anyone, not even to *Stern*. In addition, Heidemann would have to be patient. For reasons not made clear by Fischer, he would stagger the delivery of the diaries, rather than handing them over in a single batch. The diaries would arrive one at a time, weeks or even months apart.

The deal seemed solid enough; the conditions acceptable. Heidemann dreamt of the money that would pass through his hands and the glory that would be his when the diaries were published. The magazine's editors imagined huge profits when circulation spiked and the rights were sold to other publishers around the world.

In their quest for glory and riches, neither party bothered to ask important questions or to investigate further.

The first volume was delivered in January 1981. Fischer passed it to Heidemann, who delivered it to *Stern*. Eager to acquire it, *Stern* accepted the diary without much scrutiny and paid Heidemann the first installment. Heidemann secretly kept a portion of the money for himself and gave the rest to Fischer.

Soon other Hitler diaries trickled into *Stern*'s hands. Then to the delight of the publisher and Heidemann, Fischer announced that his early figures had been wrong. There were more than twenty-seven diaries, there were at least sixty-two. *Stern* increased its payout. Millions more passed from hand to hand, with Heidemann secretly taking a cut before passing Fischer his share.

Before offering the rights to other publishers, *Stern* took a precautionary step. Figuring that other publishers would want to know that the diaries were authentic before shelling out money, *Stern* hired three handwriting experts. They were given photocopies of pages from the first diary and, for comparison, samples of Hitler's own handwriting retrieved from the German Federal Archives. After some study, the experts announced their findings. The handwriting matched. The diaries were authentic. They had been written by Hitler.

Adolf Hitler poses with a group of SS members
soon after his appointment as Chancellor.

News of the discovery broke. In the days that followed, *Stern* published excerpts. There was a wave of excitement, followed by an onslaught of criticism. Something was not quite right with the diaries, skeptics said. Ideas expressed on the pages differed from historical records at times. There were errors in places, too, and the language lacked Hitler's usual flair.

Stern defended its position and proceeded with its plans to publish the diaries, but the debate prompted the West German Federal Archives to conduct a scientific investigation. The diaries were inspected by several forensic experts. Chemists conducted tests on the paper, bindings and ink.

Other experts re-examined the handwriting's loops and swirls, the slant and slope of the letters, and the size of spaces between words. They compared these to legitimate samples of Hitler's writing. Language specialists read passages to see if the style and voice were consistent with other writings by Hitler. At the same time, historians analyzed the ideas and opinions in the text to see if they matched up with Hitler's actions and decisions.

On May 6, 1983, only hours before *Stern* was scheduled to publish the diaries, the West German Federal Archives announced its findings. Chemical tests showed that the ink was no more than twelve months old and that the paper had been treated with a brightener not used before 1954. The bindings contained the same brightener as well as threads of polyester, a synthetic substance produced only after World War II.

Language experts and historians found discrepancies, too. The Hitler portrayed in the diaries was more gentle and tolerant than the real Hitler had been. There were gaps in the writing — details that seemed to be missing, famous names left out. Some of the passages had been lifted word-for-word from other books published about Hitler, including mistakes in facts, grammar and spelling.

The new panel of handwriting experts agreed that the diaries had been written by someone other than Hitler. But their investigation revealed something else, too — that *Stern*'s handwriting experts had not been completely wrong. The handwriting in the diaries *did* match the handwriting in the documents taken from the German Federal Archives. What the original experts didn't know was that *those* documents had not been written by Hitler. They had been forged, too. Unwittingly the handwriting experts had compared one forgery with another written by the same person.

The final verdict was clear. Without a doubt, the diaries were fakes. In the words of Dr. Louis-Ferdinand Werner, who supervised the chemical analysis, "It's very simple. When the paper's been manufactured later, then the volumes cannot be genuine."

By this time, 5 to 10 million German marks had trickled out of *Stern*'s hands. *Stern* had been duped. Heidemann, too. But how had Fischer managed to swindle both in such a clever way?

As it turned out, Konrad Fischer was an alias used by Konrad Kujau, a dealer in Nazi memorabilia. Kujau manufactured many of the items that he sold. He falsified documents, forged signatures, added emblems and swastikas to commonplace objects, and blended facts with fanciful tales — whatever it took to attract buyers and increase sales.

Anything written by Hitler or bearing his signature was especially valuable. With *Stern* willing to pay exorbitant amounts, Kujau swung into high gear, cranking out volume after volume. To create the diaries, he started with notebooks that had black covers and blank pages. Using black ink, he wrote in a carefully scripted style. To make the words sound Hitler-like, Kujau borrowed quotes from reference books, newspapers and medical records. By pouring tea on the pages, he gave them an aged appearance. Slapping the pages together and smacking them against a table added to their weathered look. To make them seem authentic, Kujau affixed two red wax seals in the form of German eagles on the covers.

After the West German Federal Archives announced its findings, Konrad Kujau was arrested and charged with forging the diaries. Eventually he confessed to the crime, but he added a twist to his story when he discovered that Heidemann had been pocketing some of the money. He claimed that Heidemann knew that the diaries were forgeries all along.

To settle the matter, the case was brought to court. Both parties were found guilty. Kujau and Heidemann were sentenced to four and a half years in prison. For its part, *Stern* was given a severe reprimand. By not investigating the diaries thoroughly from the beginning, the publisher had been naïve, negligent and essentially an accomplice to the plot, the court said.

As for the missing millions, Kujau claimed that Heidemann had the bulk of it. Heidemann claimed that most of it was in Kujau's pockets. Wherever it was, the money seemed to have simply disappeared.

UNPROVEN ════════════════════════

The Skull of Mozart

For decades, a partial skull was on display at the Mozarteum University in Salzburg, Austria. To many music lovers, the yellowish bones were the genuine thing — the skull of the great composer Wolfgang Amadeus Mozart. Others doubted the claim.

There were good reasons for doubt. When Mozart died on December 5, 1791, his body was buried in an unmarked grave. Ten years later, a gravedigger unearthed a skull. Believing it was Mozart's, he passed it on to the composer's family. In 1902, Mozart's relatives donated it to the Mozarteum. The authenticity of the skull has been questioned ever since.

In 2006, as the two hundred and fiftieth anniversary of Mozart's birth neared, a scientific study was conducted to decide if the skull was his. A physical examination of the bones provided some encouraging proof. The teeth had tiny holes, suggesting rickets, a disease of the bones that Mozart had as a boy. There was also evidence of tooth decay; Mozart had complained of constant toothaches during his short life. Also convincing was a fracture on the left side of the skull that was consistent with a blow to the head Mozart had suffered in a carriage accident a year before he died.

Less convincing, however, was the DNA evidence. When mito-chondrial DNA extracted from the skull's teeth was compared to that from Mozart's niece and maternal grandmother, scientists were left with more questions than answers. Unlike regular DNA, which is inherited from both parents, mitochondrial DNA is passed unchanged along the female line of the family and con-tains the genetic blueprint of only one parent, the mother.

No DNA connection was found between the skull and Mozart's female relatives. Surprising, too, was that there was no DNA connection between Mozart's niece and his grandmother.

Judging by the DNA results, either the skull belongs to someone else, or the two "relatives" used for comparison are not from Mozart's family at all. Although the skull might still be his, proof — at least for now — remains elusive.

The Case of the Deadly Inferno

The wildfire spread, consuming forests and killing firefighters. Could the arsonist be caught before striking again?

The Esperanza wildfire near Cabazon, California, started small. When first spotted in the early morning on October 26, 2006, it was barely an orange glow in the forest. Fed by tinder and dry brush and fanned by California's fierce Santa Ana winds, the fire quickly spread. Flames swooped up the San Jacinto Mountains, outrunning wildlife, turning homes into infernos and forcing the evacuation of hundreds.

Fire crews from the U.S. Forest Service were dispatched. Trained and experienced, the firefighters knew the enemy. They understood fire's appetite, its need for fuel and oxygen to stay alive. Take away one or both and fire loses power. The firefighters also knew fire's unpredictable ways. How superheated trees can explode like cannons, shooting fiery missiles. How flames can leap 15 metres across gaps in the forest. How shifts in wind can change fire's direction in a heartbeat.

Five firefighters from Engine 57 were dispatched to a steep canyon above Cabazon to defend a vacant, partially built house. Shortly after 8 a.m., the wind shifted, blowing fire toward them. There wasn't time to react. In minutes, flames rolled over the crew. Two of the men died next to their fire engine, another near the building. The other two firefighters died shortly after, their injuries too severe.

Reeling from shock, the remaining firefighters doubled their efforts, but as the day wore on an ugly truth became apparent. The Esperanza fire was not the only one in the San Jacinto

Mountains. At 4:11 the same morning a second fire had been spotted, at 7:30, a third, and by late afternoon, a fourth.

Because of the clear skies that night, lightning was ruled out as a cause. Nor were the fires thought to be accidental. They were too frequent, too clustered together to be the result of a carelessly dropped match or cigarette. The fires had been purposely set, the work of one or more arsonists. Only now, with the deaths of five firefighters, more than arson was involved. Murder was, too.

As the fire continued to rage the following day, a state of emergency was declared. Firefighters from surrounding areas were called to action. Three days later the fire was finally contained. By then it had consumed 163 square kilometres and destroyed thirty-four houses and twenty outbuildings.

The wildfire set by an arsonist and driven by fierce Santa Ana winds killed five federal firefighters and drove hundreds of people from their homes.

Immediately after the fire was squelched, investigators combed the scorched ground, searching for clues that would help capture the arsonist. First they had to locate the fire's starting point. Intense heat destroys much of the surface growth, but fire investigators are skilled at reading subtle indicators left behind. To their trained eyes, each blackened root, soot-stained rock or collapsed building tells a story about the fire's intensity, speed and movement. Unevenly charred tree trunks, for example, indicate where heat intensity was greatest. Singed grasses, folded at the base, lie in the direction of the fire that consumed them. Shocked into alignment by the heat, pine needles also point like fingers to the source.

Also available to forensic experts were a hundred images of the fire that had been taken by NASA. Snapped at an altitude of 13,000 metres by unmanned aircraft, the visible and infrared images showed the fire's progress over a sixteen-hour period. When analyzed, the images gave investigators vital information about the fire's movement and the effect of winds and other factors on its speed and direction.

A photo of the Esperanza Fire from space helped investigators determine where the fire originated.

73

From the evidence, forensic experts mapped the fire's path and discovered its point of origin. The fire had started at the base of the mountains. Among the charred remains, investigators found the device that had started it — a bundle of matches held in place with a rubber band around a Marlboro cigarette. Called a "lay-over" by forensic experts, the bundle acted as a timer that allowed the arsonist to control the moment of ignition. Once lit, the cigarette burned slowly until it reached the matches and ignited them, creating a flare-up. The delayed reaction also gave the arsonist time to leave the area.

The match bundle was the arsonist's signature, and investigators had seen this device before.

Was he the killer who had caused the deaths of five firefighters?

In the few months prior, there had been a rash of wildfires. Since May over fifty fires had been started in the area, many with lay-over devices similar to the one used in the Esperanza fire.

Arsonists often revisit their fires to watch as flames grab hold and spread. Believing that a serial arsonist might be at work, police had set up surveillance cameras atop utility poles. Four days before the Esperanza fire, a Ford Taurus had been recorded entering a remote canyon within minutes of a fire there. The car belonged to Raymond Lee Oyler, a thirty-six-year-old mechanic. When police searched Oyler's vehicle they found a wig, latex gloves, cigarettes, black spray paint, a partly burned slingshot and a book that outlined, among other things, how to make fire starters similar to the lay-over device.

A police investigation uncovered other evidence linking

Oyler to the fires. Tire tracks from the Taurus matched those found at another site. Oyler smoked cigarettes and preferred Marlboros. Chemical tests on the matches recovered from some of the lay-over devices showed that they were identical to each other and had come from the same box. The matches were also identical to those found at the home of Oyler's fiancée's mother. Furthermore, when the fires were plotted on a map, Oyler's apartment was right in the centre.

Oyler was arrested. Although police believed he was responsible for many of the fires, they only had evidence to charge him with the fires of June 9 and 10. The charges were enough, though, to hold Oyler in custody while police investigated further.

Had Oyler also started the Esperanza fire? Was he the killer who had caused the deaths of five firefighters? To link Oyler to the Esperanza fire, solid evidence was needed.

Microscopic and hidden, the evidence was there, waiting to be found. Investigators had the charred remains of two lay-over devices used in the June fires. After Oyler's arrest, biochemists extracted DNA from saliva deposited on the cigarettes of each device. They compared it to Oyler's DNA and it matched, linking him to the earlier fires. Further analysis showed that Oyler's DNA also matched DNA extracted from the cigarette that started the Esperanza blaze.

Oyler was charged with five counts of first-degree murder, twenty-two counts of arson and seventeen counts of using incendiary devices to start fires in the area where he lived. At the trial, evidence was presented to a jury. Witnesses testified that Oyler had talked about setting fires. A truck driver at a gas station said that shortly after the Esperanza fire started, Oyler had told him the fire "is happening just the way I thought it would."

Experts were brought into court armed with data to show that Oyler had time, motive and opportunity to set the Esperanza fire. On the day of the fire, he had started work at 7:52 a.m. By then the Esperanza fire was fully engaged and two of the three other fires had already been set. Circumstantial evidence connecting Oyler to the fires was also presented — a slingshot found in the Taurus that was likely used to launch the lay-over device; tire impressions taken from one fire scene; video of Oyler's car leaving another.

He had left physical evidence as good as a fingerprint.

Of all the evidence, though, the most compelling was the DNA extracted from the cigarette left at the crime scene. To start the Esperanza fire, Oyler had ignited the cigarette, puffing on it to nurse it to life. In doing so, he had left physical evidence as good as a fingerprint. Surviving heat and flames, the DNA in his saliva showed that he had started the blaze.

After a week of deliberation, the jury returned a verdict of murder against Olyer. On June 5, 2009, he was sentenced to death for the crime.

Scientists Find the Answers

• *How did day turn to night?*
Written accounts describing the so-called "Dark Day" say that by noon of May 19, 1780, the sky over the New England states was so dark that flowers folded their petals, night birds began to sing and people ate their midday meals by candlelight. For nearly 230 years, the cause of the darkness was a mystery. In 2008, research scientists at the Tree Ring Laboratory at the University of Missouri solved the case by studying trees. Tree rings dating to 1780 contained charcoal, resin and other residues, clear signs that a massive wildfire had swept through the region. Scientists believe that winds carried the smoke southeast, darkening the sky and producing the "day into night" effect.

• *Getting the perfect sound*
Whether sitting in the front row or at the back of the 2500-year-old Theatre of Epidaurus near Athens, Greece, the effect is much the same — near-perfect sound from any seat. How such superior sound quality was achieved in ancient times has been a long-standing mystery. In 2007, acoustical researchers led by ultrasonics expert Nico Declercq of the Georgia Institute of Technology unravelled the secret. By experimenting with ultrasonic waves and computer simulations of the theatre's acoustics, they isolated the factors that influenced the sound. They discovered that the theatre's limestone seats acted as natural filters, smothering lower frequencies of sound like crowd noises, but allowing higher frequency sounds like the actors' voices to be transmitted freely. Another mystery yet to be solved — was the design feature intentional or an accident?

- *East to west or west to east?*

How the Polynesian Islands of the South Pacific became inhabited was widely debated in the 1930s. After observing that wind and ocean currents generally travel in easterly directions, Norwegian anthropologist Thor Heyerdahl proposed that the earliest settlers could have come from South America in primitive boats. In 1947, Heyerdahl and a crew of five inexperienced sailors used ancient building methods to construct an 11-metre raft from balsa logs, a raft that they called the *Kon-Tiki*. Setting sail from Callào, Peru, the men arrived in the Polynesian Islands 101 days later, an 8000-kilometre journey that proved Heyerdahl's theory: it was possible for Polynesia's earliest inhabitants to have come from South America.

CHAPTER 3
EXPLAIN

Introduction

The body in front of Dr. Frank Ruhli was more bone than flesh. Brown leathery skin covered shrivelled muscles. The arms and legs were almost skeletal. Patches of fuzz clung to the skull and the face was expressionless. Death seemed to have been sudden. But what was the cause? Why did the man die?

All things considered, the body was in fine shape. It was the perfect specimen for Ruhli, a Swiss pathologist with a unique specialty. While most pathologists examine the freshly dead, Ruhli's subjects are mummies that are hundreds, even thousands, of years old.

This mummy was one of the world's oldest and most famous. Nicknamed Otzi the Iceman, it was discovered in 1991 high in the Italian Alps. Since then, the mummy has been examined by dozens of scientists. Fascinating facts about Otzi's life had emerged. So had puzzling questions about his death.

Otzi was about forty-five years old when he died around five thousand years ago. Overall he appears to have been in good health — strong, fit and used to long hikes in the mountains. There didn't seem to be any obvious reasons for his death. How then did it happen?

There were theories from the start. Perhaps Otzi had died of exposure after becoming trapped in a winter storm? Or maybe he'd fallen and died of his injuries?

In 2001, X-rays and CT scans showed something that hadn't been noticed earlier — an arrowhead lodged in Otzi's left shoulder. More research found that the shaft of the arrow had been removed before death and there were bruises and cuts to his hands, wrist and chest. Otzi's skull showed signs of trauma, too.

Based on the new evidence, Otzi's death seemed to have been more violent than originally thought. Before exploring the new theories, proof was needed that the arrow had caused the Iceman's death.

Ruhli was invited to the South Tyrol Museum of Archaeology in Bolzano, Italy, where Otzi was stored. Using advanced CT scanning methods and newly developed magnetic resonance imaging (MRI) techniques, Ruhli looked inside the mummy. Scans of the left shoulder area showed that a major artery had been punctured by the arrow. Around the surrounding tissue, a large blood clot was visible.

Ruhli concluded that Otzi's death had been a direct result of the injury. When struck by the arrow, an artery had been pierced. Blood had flowed into the soft tissue. The massive bleeding had produced shock and then heart failure. "He would not have walked around for days," Ruhli said. "It was a quick death."

While the exact circumstances behind Otzi's death are still being studied, this case and others in this chapter illustrate how scientists work. Evidence, carefully gathered, analyzed and weighed, leads to speculation and potential explanations. When more advanced technologies or more intensive examinations reveal new evidence, earlier theories are reassessed. Sometimes a simple fine-tuning is all that is needed, a small adjustment of the explanation to match the new evidence. Other times, the original explanation might be too weak or inaccurate to survive such scrutiny. In that situation, an entirely new one might arise to take its place.

The Case of the Missing Ships and Desperate Sailors

Clues scattered across the Arctic told a tragic tale of frantic and confused men struggling to survive. What happened to the Franklin expedition?

In 1845, two ships sailed from England in search of an open-water passage through the Arctic. The ships and the sailors aboard never returned. They disappeared with scarcely a trace and barely an explanation. Gone were the *Terror* and the *Erebus*, two well-equipped, steam-driven wooden vessels. Gone, too, were the experienced commander of the expedition, Sir John Franklin, his entire crew of 128 men, and supplies to last three or more years.

Numerous investigations were launched to unravel the mystery of the expedition's fate.

Despite over 160 years of searching in the Canadian Arctic, only a few scattered remnants of the expedition have ever been found — three marked graves on tiny Beechey Island, leftovers of a winter camp on King William Island, an abandoned lifeboat, a few tin cans, the occasional tool, the odd weapon, some books, a couple of scrawled notes and a smattering of human bones.

The sparse evidence tells a haunting story of ships that became locked in crushing ice and of desperate men who abandoned their sinking vessels. Pushing lifeboats filled with supplies across the ice, the exhausted sailors tried to escape to the mainland. Weak and hungry, stricken with pneumonia and other diseases, one by one they collapsed and died.

But there are nagging questions about the decisions made by

Franklin and his men. Some of their choices seem risky, even foolish and doomed to failure from the start. Why did they behave in such an irrational way? What became of the ships and the men?

In the summers of 1981 and 1982, a team of scientists led by Owen Beattie, an anthropologist from the University of Alberta, visited King William Island in the Canadian Arctic. There the team found stray pieces of clothing, wood and rope. At Booth Point on the island's southern shore, researchers found a cluster of thirty-one human bone fragments, the remains of a Franklin expedition crew member.

A physical examination of the bones showed they were pitted and scaled, signs of Vitamin C deficiency, the cause of scurvy. But the researchers also found scrapes and cuts on the bones that indicated knives had been used to cut through the flesh. To them this meant one thing: the crew had resorted to a desperate act to survive — cannibalism.

Too much lead in the body acts as a poison. If enough lead is present, death is a possibility.

The bones were sent to the Alberta Soil and Feed Testing Laboratory in Edmonton, where another discovery was made. There was an extremely high concentration of lead in them. Too much lead in the body acts as a poison. A person suffering from lead poisoning becomes weak and tired, may behave strangely, become irritable, be unable to work well with others and be prone to simple mistakes in judgment. If enough lead is present, death is a possibility.

Believing lead poisoning might explain the crew's behaviour, Beattie embarked on a second investigation. The bone fragments showed that lead had accumulated in one body over a lifetime. They didn't prove, however, that the lead had entered the body during the expedition. That kind of proof could only come from tissue and hair samples, which showed fresh growth over a shorter time period.

Beattie and a team of experts flew to Beechey Island. There they found the wooden markers that stood over the graves of three sailors who had died in the expedition's first winter.

Beattie had government permission to unearth the bodies, take X-rays, perform autopsies, collect tissue samples and then return the bodies to their graves. He decided to start with John Torrington, the first man to die on the expedition. To ensure that everything would be returned to its original state, the grave was carefully staked. Using trowels, pickaxes and shovels, layers of gravel and permafrost were gradually chipped away. Progress was slow, hampered by rock-hard ice that had cemented the stones together. After two full days of digging, the team could see the lid of Torrington's coffin.

The coffin was filled with ice. To melt it, warm water was poured inside. At first only a dim patch of blue could be seen underneath, but as more of the ice melted, a body wrapped in navy-coloured fabric became visible. When all of the fabric was finally free, it was pulled back to reveal a face, eyes half-closed as if waking from a long sleep, mouth partly open as if to speak.

Nearly fourteen decades had passed since the burial, but John Torrington looked almost as he did when he had died on January 1, 1846. The frozen ground of the far North had preserved his body. He wore a striped cotton shirt and pants, but no shoes or boots. Strips of cloth had been tied around him to hold his arms, legs and chin in place. The flesh was tinged blue, the result of dye seeping from the fabric that covered him.

The body was carefully lifted out of the grave and laid on the ground. A physical examination showed he had no wounds or obvious signs of illness. An autopsy was conducted and samples of bone, hair and brain tissue were collected. Then the body was photographed, placed back in the coffin and reburied.

Because summer was drawing to a close, there wasn't time to open the other graves, but two years later the team returned to complete their work. Like Torrington's, the bodies of John Hartnell and William Braine were well preserved. Braine's grave was particularly strange. His arms, body and head were carelessly positioned and his undershirt was on backwards. The coffin lid was pressing down on his nose, as if the coffin was too small to fit him properly. Braine's burial seemed to have been a hasty affair, suggesting that by the time of his death the crew had also been weakened by starvation and disease.

The body of able seaman John Hartnell, a member of Franklin's expedition, is reburied in the permafrost on Beechey Island, Nunavut, in 1986.

As with Torrington, the bodies were examined, X-rays were taken and autopsies were done. Samples of hair and tissue were collected and the corpses were reburied.

Laboratory tests on the tissue samples showed that all three men had been exposed to lead poisoning during the expedition.

To Beattie there was one strong possibility to explain where the lead originated. Most of the food eaten during Franklin's voyage had been preserved in tin cans, a relatively new innovation at the time. Although the tin itself would not cause lead poisoning, the lead solder holding the seams together might have. Beattie believed the lead could have seeped into the food and, over the long voyage, gradually poisoned the men.

In 1992, archaeologists and anthropologists on King William Island unearthed nearly four hundred bones and bone fragments as well as clay pipes, buttons, brass fittings and other artifacts from the expedition. When forensic anthropologist Anne Keenleyside examined the bones, she found cut marks similar to the ones found by Beattie. These bones tested high for lead as well.

While scientists and historians generally agree that lead poisoning affected the judgment and health of the crew, not everyone believes that the lethal dose came from the tinned food alone. In 2008, William Battersby, a British archaeologist, proposed something quite different. Through research, he uncovered another possible source. Before leaving England, the *Erebus* and *Terror* were equipped with new, one-of-a-kind water supply systems. Since lead pipes and lead solder were common plumbing materials at the time, Battersby believes they might have introduced lead into the ship's drinking water.

Proof for Battersby's theory may not be far off. There is good reason to believe that the *Erebus* and *Terror* will eventually be found. Not only have changes in Arctic climate allowed for longer ice-free periods to search, but there have also been fresh clues discovered in recent years. Some of these have come, not from science, but from Inuit storytellers.

Louie Kamoukak, an Inuit researcher, and Dorothy Harley Eber, a Montreal journalist who spent forty years interviewing Inuit elders, have collected stories about events from long ago. One account tells of a ship that became locked in ice just off the Royal Geographical Society Islands in the winter of 1850. The story mentions starving, desperate men staggering through the snow, too proud to ask local Inuit for help.

Greasy deposits along the shoreline have also been discovered, which may be proof of the Inuit stories. Possibly these are the remains of fire pits used by stranded crew to burn seal oil blubber for cooking and warmth. Also recovered were snippets of copper sheathing that might be bits of the protective plating that covered *Terror*'s hull.

In 2008, Parks Canada began a search for Franklin's ships, headed by senior archeologist Robert Grenier. Following the trail of clues, the team centered on a stretch of water between O'Reilly and Kirkwall Islands, a region pinpointed by the Inuit. Although the search was discontinued the following year, there are hopes that it will be resumed in the near future.

Meanwhile Grenier holds his own theories about what happened onboard the *Erebus* and the *Terror*. He believes that, contrary to nineteenth-century accounts, not all of the crew abandoned the ice-locked vessels. At least two crew members remained aboard, drifting with the ships as the ice carried them southward, and staying with them until they finally sank. Grenier's theory is backed by stories told by Inuit hunters who arrived on the scene. According to the stories, the hunters found one ship destroyed and another still floating, with a tall dead man lying on deck. The last surviving ship, Grenier believes, was the *Terror,* and the copper bits recovered nearby were salvaged from her hull by Inuit who boarded the vessel.

Today, at McMaster University in Hamilton, Ontario, researchers with the Department of Anthropology are testing canning methods from the 1840s. Using lead-soldered cans similar to those carried by the Franklin expedition, a modern-day batch of ox-cheek soup will eventually be opened and analyzed for lead content. Results may show how quickly lead leached into the food supply, rendering it lethal.

In another study, Bruno Tremblay, an ocean scientist with Montreal's McGill University, has installed monitoring buoys in key spots along Franklin's final route. By charting currents, water temperature, underwater sounds and other data, he hopes to determine prevailing conditions at the time of Franklin's voyage, data that could pinpoint the ships' location.

New scientific techniques are helping, too. In 1869, a body found on King William Island was identified by English doctors as Henry le Vesconte, one of the officers. In 2011, thanks to a reconstruction of the dead man's face and a chemical probe of his teeth, scientists proved that it was likely a different officer: Harry Goodsir, the expedition's naturalist and assistant surgeon.

Each scientific improvement and new piece of evidence offers hope that the Franklin mystery will eventually be solved. For now, though, it remains very much an open case, a puzzle with more questions than answers.

EXPLAINED

Herculaneum's Missing Citizens

On August 24, A.D. 79, Italy's Mount Vesuvius erupted, smothering the city of Pompeii and burying the seaside port of Herculaneum. In the centuries that followed, the once-thriving cities were forgotten.

In 1709, Herculaneum was rediscovered by workers digging a well. Soon archaeologists and anthropologists were chipping away at the rock, revealing life as it was centuries ago. Unlike Pompeii, where most of the buildings had collapsed, Herculaneum was largely intact, frozen in time by the sudden eruption. Kitchen shelves were stacked with dishes; dinner plates were filled with food; doors stood open as if occupants had just stepped out.

One curiosity soon surfaced. Only nine skeletons were found in the buried city. The theory was that the other residents had escaped by fleeing in boats or by foot along mountain trails. The few that had died, it was thought, suffocated on enormous amounts of ash spewed by the volcano.

In 1980, two skeletons were discovered on Herculaneum's ancient beach. One was found next to an overturned boat. Two years later, thirteen more skeletons were uncovered, and since then almost two hundred others. Many of the victims were huddled together, some in contorted positions, jaws open, arms and legs flailing.

The discoveries at Herculaneum painted a new picture of the town's final day. Rather than escaping, many of the citizens died trying to reach the boats. The cause of their death was not suffocation, but thermal shock when temperatures soared close to 540° Celsius. Muscles contracted, lungs collapsed and skin vaporized. Moments later, boiling ash and mud swallowed the bodies, preserving the tortured last moments of the fleeing residents.

The Case of the Mountain Mummies

Head resting on his knees, arms wrapped around his legs, the boy looked peacefully asleep, but it was clear there was more to his story.

On the high reaches of the South American Andes, the air is thin, the slope steep. The wind often whips across the mountains with hurricane forces. Altitude sickness, constant exhaustion and gripping sub-zero temperatures challenge those who dare to make the climb.

In 1954, two men braved the severe conditions and climbed El Plomo, a 5000-metre mountain near Santiago, Chile. They were seeking gold and silver treasure — relics of the Inca, a powerful empire that once ruled the high Andes. Sold to the highest bidder, these items could earn the men a small fortune.

Near the mountain peak the men found three small rectangular buildings, and inside the largest one, a flat stone on the dirt floor. After prying it loose, they slid it aside. Freezing air spilled from the cavity below. The men saw splatters of colour, then, as their eyes grew accustomed to the darkness, something else. The body of a small boy.

The boy looked to be eight or nine years old. He sat huddled, head resting on his knees, arms wrapped around his legs, his left hand clutching his right. A wool headband held a crest of black and white condor feathers in place. He wore leather fur-trimmed moccasins and a black tunic decorated with red fringe. His face had been painted red with yellow stripes and his long hair had been carefully arranged in fine braids. The boy looked peacefully asleep, but from his clothing and the objects in the tomb it appeared that he had been dead for many years, frozen in position all this time.

Believing the mummy might be sold to an interested buyer,

the two men notified officials at the National Museum of Natural History in Santiago. Officials purchased the body and other artifacts for the museum.

The discovery of a mummy in the high Andes sparked an intense archaeological investigation. Who was the child? How did he come to be buried in this lonely tomb?

He had been alive when he entered the tomb.

Fortunately there were clues. The black woollen tunic, condor-feather headdress and silver ornaments suggested the boy was an Inca, possibly from the Altiplano tribe that had inhabited the mountain region five hundred years ago. Likely he had been the son of a noble or other wealthy tribe member. Tissue samples, X-rays and measurements of the body showed that the boy had been well nourished and healthy. Scientists confirmed that he had been alive when he entered the tomb, but soon died from exposure to sub-zero temperatures.

It was obvious that the boy had not been thoughtlessly dumped in the pit. A ritual had been followed. His face had been painted red, a colour the Incas used in special ceremonies. His hair had been carefully combed and braided. Several pouches found with the boy were filled with souvenirs of his life: human hair, nail cuttings, baby teeth and pieces of red wool. Two other pouches were packed with coca leaves to deaden his hunger and cold. The boy's feet were covered in heavy calluses, which suggested that he had walked a great distance. Yet his moccasins were new.

More clues came from the mountain itself. Two sets of buildings were located. The first set — the three rectangular buildings found by the men — was located close to the peak.

A second building, a temple, was located lower down. All the buildings were aligned in the same direction.

With the information provided by the body, the artifacts and the site, archaeologists began to piece together a story of the boy's final days. The young boy had been the victim of human sacrifice. Carefully dressed, face painted, hair plaited, and with new moccasins on his well-travelled feet, the boy had probably been led from the temple to the rectangular building near the summit after a ceremony. He had been placed into the hole in the floor and the slab of rock slid into place. Drugged with a potion of chicha beer and armed with coca leaves to ward off pain, he sat huddled to conserve warmth. Knees drawn to his chest, left hand clutching his right, head leaning to one side, the boy died in this position, a human sacrifice to the gods from the Inca.

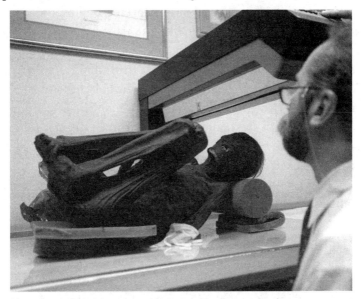

A scientist scans a thousand-year-old mummy with a dual-X-ray bone densitometer.

The discovery of the El Plomo mummy caused a stir among scientists and historians. Sixteenth-century Spanish explorers had written about Inca ceremonies called *Capacocha* in which children were sacrificed, sometimes in brutal ways. The stories were believed to be largely untrue — exaggerated accounts of much tamer Inca practices. The discovery of the El Plomo mummy changed these views. It verified that *Capacocha* really existed, though the exact reasons for the practice were still not known.

Since then more than 115 sacred Inca ceremonial sites have now been located on Andean peaks from central Chile to southern Peru. Over thirty-five mummies of children — both boys and girls — have been found in remote tombs.

Anthropologist Johan Reinhard has spent three decades exploring Andean peaks and has discovered well over a dozen *Capacocha* mummies. In 1995, he unearthed the first young female mummy on Mount Ampato in Peru. In 1999, Reinhard made another impressive discovery. At the summit of towering Mount Llullaillaco, beneath 1.5 metres of rubble, he found three mummies — two girls and a boy between eight and fifteen years old. Buried with the bodies was a wealth of artifacts: thirty-six gold and silver statues, small woven bags, a ceramic vessel, seashell necklaces and plumes of feathers.

The greatest treasure lies not in dazzling artifacts, however. Rather it is *inside* the mummies themselves, in their bones and internal organs. With modern methods such as CT scans and 3D imaging systems, it is possible to see below the skin without damaging the body. By looking inside the mummy, scientists can learn about the mummification practices of ancient cultures as well as about the health of the individual and the reasons for death. Mummies are also a source of DNA. Analysis of DNA could help determine relationships among ancient Inca tribes, their patterns of movement and even the selection process that decided which children were chosen for sacrifice. Because of these discoveries, science has helped give historians a better understanding of Inca culture and beliefs.

As cruel as *Capacocha* might seem to us today, to the ancient Inca it was likely not viewed that way. Says Reinhard: "The sacrifices were children, because they were considered to be the most pure. They were being sacrificed to enter the real world of the gods. It was considered a great honour. These children didn't die in the sense that we think. They went to live in a paradise with the gods . . . It was a transition into a better life . . . "

TOOLS

CT Scan (Computerized Axial Tomography)

In a CT scan (or CAT scan as it is sometimes called), X-rays are taken from many angles to produce a series of cross-sectional images of an object's interior. The data is transmitted to a computer which builds a 3D picture from the separate X-rays. If, for example, a loaf of raisin bread was the object, an X-ray would show the inside of the whole loaf. The image would appear flat, and there would be no depth to show whether one raisin was in front or behind another. With a CT scan, the inside of the loaf could be seen one slice at a time, and the location of each raisin would appear in its exact position in space.

The Case of the Desert Shipwreck

With each shovelful of sand, the mystery grew. So did the questions. An ancient ship in the desert? Whose was it? What was it doing there?

Scratch the desert surface along the southern coast of Namibia, Africa, and precious stones seem to magically appear. But while diamonds might be common in this area, copper ingots are not. In 2008, Bob Burrell, a geologist doing a survey of the region for the De Beers Mining Company, spotted a nugget-sized half-sphere of copper in the sand. Stamped on the weathered ingot was a three-pronged fork — a trident.

Immediately, the ingot aroused the interest of archeologists. The object was man-made and looked old. The trident was the official logo of a merchant, and the ingot had once been used as currency for his purchases and trade.

A Spanish gold coin, three Portuguese silver coins and a pair of brass dividers from a shipwreck off the southwest coast of Namibia.

The discovery fuelled an investigation. Archaeologists sectioned off the site, scanned it with lasers, and dug deep into the sand, measuring and photographing. They found thousands of copper ingots stamped with the distinctive trident, most brown or black, some tinged green with age — 19 metric tonnes in all. Also found were two thousand gold coins — mostly Spanish, but a number of Venetian, Moorish, French and Portuguese coins as well. There were other artifacts, too — cannons, swords, muskets, wooden masts, tattered sails and tangled rigging — evidence of a mangled ship whose wreckage had been scattered. Among the stranger items uncovered were human toe bones wedged inside a ragged shoe. Also strange was the discovery 5 kilometres farther up the coast of a huge wooden rigging block.

Dubbed the Diamond Shipwreck, this was the oldest shipwreck ever discovered along the coast of sub-Saharan Africa, and the richest. But with each shovelful of sand, the mystery grew. So did the questions: An ancient ship in the desert? Whose was it? What was it doing there?

From the number of coins the vessel carried, it seemed certain that the ship had been on a trading mission. In the sixteenth century, European vessels regularly sailed down the African coast and skirted the Cape of Good Hope, the storm-riddled tip of Africa. From there they steered across the Indian Ocean. Their goal was to reach India, a country teeming with spices, tea, finely woven fabrics and other items highly prized in Europe.

Archaeologists turned to European archives for answers. They found that the trident was the mark of Anton Fugger, a German merchant and one of the sixteenth century's wealthiest financiers. Along with coins, the copper ingots were the currency of their day. The ship was also carrying large numbers of coins from different countries. Quite likely it had been on its way to purchase goods in India, but never made it.

Bruno Werz of the Southern African Institute of Maritime Archaeological Research poses with two of the astrolabes found near the Namibia wreck.

The distinctive style of the ship, its contours and construction as well as its cargo, suggested that it was a Portuguese vessel. Unfortunately, Portuguese shipping records were almost non-existent. In 1755, natural disasters had destroyed most of Lisbon and sent the building that housed Portugal's shipping records sliding into a nearby river.

Fortunately, there were plenty of coins to provide a time frame. Spanish coins were the most common. These were stamped with the figures of King Ferdinand and Queen Isabella, Spanish rulers in the late fifteenth and early sixteenth centuries.

The Portuguese coins were stamped with the coat of arms of João III, a king who ruled Portugal in the first half of the sixteenth century.

The King João coins were particularly rare. They had been minted for only a few years, from 1525 to 1538. Afterwards the coins had been recalled, melted and recast into other forms. That so many King João coins had escaped the recall suggested that the ship had been at sea — or even lost — during that thirteen-year period. With the time frame narrowed, the search for the ship's identity intensified.

Alexandre Monteiro, a Portuguese maritime archaeologist and researcher, found a book called the *Relações das Armadas* that described Portugal's shipping fleets of the era. A careful reading of the book showed that while numerous ships had sailed to India between 1525 and 1600, only twenty-one had been lost. Out of those, only one Portuguese ship had gone down near Namibia — the *Bom Jesus* (the *Good Jesus*). The date it sailed was 1533.

Monteiro discovered other documents, too. In one report, Captain Dom João Pereira had filed an account of a voyage in which he mentioned the loss of the *Bom Jesus* in a wild storm near the Cape. Another source, a rare book from the sixteenth century, included an illustration of a double-masted ship, sails unfurled, bow dipping into the waves. Dated 1533, the illustration was accompanied by a caption: *Bom Jesus: perdido* — lost.

The wreck beneath Namibia's desert now had an identity — the *Bom Jesus*. It had gone down in a violent storm in 1533 near the Cape of Good Hope.

Archaeologists and historians are still at work, sifting through evidence, reconstructing the story of the *Bom Jesus*. Although there is still much to do, based upon what has been discovered so far, they have a likely story of the ship's final voyage.

Four months after sailing from Lisbon, after weeks of visiting ports along the African coast, the *Bom Jesus* neared the Cape of Good Hope. Powerful winds lashed the ship and whipped the ocean into frothy waves. Bloated with riches, the *Bom Jesus* rose with the swells and dipped with the troughs. Fearing for their lives, the sailors had strapped themselves to masts or cowered below deck.

Separated from the rest of the fleet and trapped in winds and currents that pushed it hundreds of kilometres north, the *Bom Jesus* was driven off course. Impossible to steer, the ship was at the mercy of high waves. Masts broken, sails shredded, the wreck was thrust toward the Namibian coast, past the normal shoreline, pushed by the current and carried by surf far higher than normal. About 150 metres inland, the ship struck a jagged rock or outcropping. Its hull opened. A chunk of stern tore off. In short order, the *Bom Jesus* was in pieces. Its three hundred crew members and passengers were scattered or drowned, its cargo lodged in sand, its wreckage strewn around the desert.

Over time, wind and waves erased all signs of the vessel and buried it under 7 metres of sand. And so it stayed for hundreds of years, until the forces of nature exposed one of Anton Fugger's ingots and a curious geologist found it.

The Curious Case of Ludwig's Demise

When death finally came to Ludwig van Beethoven, it was a blessing. But it also left science with a puzzling mystery. What killed the famous composer?

Around 5:45 p.m. on March 26, 1827, Ludwig van Beethoven took his last breath. The fifty-six-year-old composer had a long history of illness. Almost completely deaf by the age of forty-two, he had suffered stomach pains, frequent depression and wild mood swings for much of his life. In his final four months, the condition worsened. Beethoven's last days were painful ones — confined to a filthy straw mattress in his Vienna apartment, his legs and back riddled with bedsores, his lungs and stomach drowning in fluid.

When it finally came, death was a blessing.

On the morning after his death, an autopsy was conducted. The top of Beethoven's skull was sawed open. The temporal bones that affected hearing were cut out and taken away for study. A cut was also made in the chest to expose the kidneys, gall bladder, spleen, stomach and other organs. The liver was as tough as leather; an awful odour filled the room.

The brain and organs were examined. Rough measurements were taken, notes scribbled. When the autopsy was over, the body was covered with a blanket and laid on long planks that rested on top of chairs. That afternoon and the next day, visitors flowed in and out of Beethoven's apartment — friends, fellow musicians and high-ranking officials, all wanting to pay their respects to the great composer.

Just before the funeral, Beethoven's body was placed in a polished oak casket, his head resting on a white silk pillow. Because

Beethoven's skull had been disfigured by the autopsy, a wreath of white roses was laid around his head to hide the damage.

Schools were closed for the funeral. Rich and poor, famous and unknown, thousands flooded the streets. The crowds were so thick, a military guard had to hold them back. Accompanied by musicians, singers and torchbearers, the coffin was carried to the church and from there to Wahring Cemetery, where it was lowered into the ground.

The crowd departed. The cemetery returned to quiet. In death, the tortured composer had finally found peace. But there was a catch . . .

One cause of Beethoven's death, the autopsy suggested, was the failure of his kidneys and liver. Beethoven had been a heavy drinker for most of his life, and large quantities of alcohol had likely deteriorated his organs. But alcohol consumption alone didn't explain everything. There seemed to be deeper, darker reasons for Beethoven's long suffering, things that the rushed autopsy couldn't explain.

As his illness worsened, Beethoven's behaviour had grown more bizarre. Once a friendly and charming man, he became hot-tempered and frequently depressed. He shut himself inside his apartment for long periods, banished his friends and yelled at visitors. When he did make an appearance, Beethoven looked haggard — his long hair uncombed, his clothes wrinkled and dirty. He roamed the streets of Vienna, head down and muttering to himself. Sometimes he flew into fits of rage, screaming at bystanders, or spitting at them for no apparent reason.

No one could explain why.

In 1863, Beethoven's body was exhumed, in order to rebury his remains in a metal casket to prevent further decomposition. It also provided an opportunity for a more thorough examination.

Thirty-two specially invited guests watched while the coffin was opened. Inside, among fragments of the rose wreath, pieces of clothing, and the sole of one shoe, were the bones of Beethoven. Beethoven's skull was in nine large pieces. Six teeth were missing; so were the temporal bones that had been removed at the autopsy and never returned.

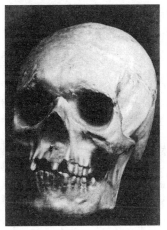

A reconstruction of Beethoven's skull.

The next day the skeleton, minus the skull, was laid out in a metal casket. To keep the vertebrae connected, the bones were tied together with string. The lid was soldered to the frame and the casket was transferred to the chapel. The skull, meanwhile, spent the night on the bedside table of Gerhard von Breuning, a prominent doctor.

In Beethoven's time, there was a strong belief in phrenology, a theory that much about a person's personality and ability could be learned by carefully examining the outside of the skull. Although we know now that what's *inside* the skull determines these things, phrenologists believed that by examining Beethoven's skull they could discover not only the cause of his illness, but also the reasons for his phenomenal musical ability.

For a week the skull was examined, measured, sketched and photographed from every angle. Plaster models were made. Each crevice or fold was searched and explored. Finally the metal casket was reopened, the skull was added and the casket closed up again. The next day Beethoven was reburied in a new vault in Wahring Cemetery, his head reunited with his body, whole once again.

For almost a century, the mystery of Beethoven's strange symptoms lingered.

But in 1888, Beethoven's remains were exhumed again, this time to bury them in a different cemetery. Twenty minutes were allowed for a quick medical examination. In the rush, nothing much was gained, except to note a curious fact. There were only seven large skull pieces in the casket, not nine as originally counted.

For almost a century, the mystery of Beethoven's strange symptoms lingered. Neither the autopsy nor the information collected during the exhumations provided many clues. Liver damage couldn't account for his bizarre behaviour. What had really ailed the composer? No one knew for certain. The answers, though, were always there, locked in two separate bits of evidence obtained long ago.

On the day after Beethoven's death, one of the visitors to the composer's apartment had been fifteen-year-old musician

Ferdinand Hiller. Hiller had clipped a lock of Beethoven's hair to take with him as a keepsake. In 1883, he gave the lock to his son, Paul, as a birthday gift. Paul had the hair sealed in a locket with a wooden frame. He also included an inscription that told the hair's origins.

The locket was passed from one generation to the next. Then in 1943, at the height of World War II, the locket was given to Kay Fremming, a doctor living in Denmark who helped save many Danish Jews from Nazi persecution. The locket stayed in the Fremming family until 1994, when it was bought at auction by four members of the American Beethoven Society, a group dedicated to preserving Beethoven's music and history.

In 1995, the locket was opened. Inside were 582 hairs, some grey, others white or brown. The hairs varied in length from 7 to 15 centimetres. Knowing that hair grows at an average rate of a centimetre per month, researchers knew that the hair in the locket provided a snapshot of the final six to twelve months of Beethoven's life.

Samples of the hair were subjected to chemical tests. Massive amounts of lead — almost one hundred times normal levels for the time — were found in Beethoven's hair. The concentrations were highest at the points where the hair grew closest to the scalp — the regions of most recent growth. Beethoven, it seemed, had been steadily exposed to lead in the final year of his illness, and even more in his last few weeks.

There was also another piece of evidence with a mysterious past and a hidden story.

After the 1863 exhumation, when the seven pieces (not nine) of Beethoven's skull were returned to the grave, several smaller fragments also went missing. Somehow the bones ended up in the skull collection of Franz Romeo Seligmann, an anthropologist who had taken measurements of the skull and was present at the reburial.

Seligmann kept the bones a secret from everyone but a few family members. He stored them in a small metal box. Now and again, someone took them out, handled them and marvelled at the wonder of holding the bones of the famous composer, but mostly the pieces were locked away for safekeeping and kept within the family.

In 1993, Paul Kaufmann of Danville, California, inherited them. Wondering if the bones really were Beethoven's, he approached scientists to find out. DNA extracted from the skull bones was compared to DNA taken from the hair in the locket. The DNA matched. The skull fragments were indeed Beethoven's.

If lead poisoning was the culprit in Beethoven's death, where did the lead come from?

Tests for lead were also done. Like the hair, the bones showed extreme levels. Since bone grows at a much slower rate than hair, and levels of lead build over time, the results showed that Beethoven had been exposed to lead much of his life, not just in the final stages of his illness. To rule out the possibility that high levels of lead might be normal for Beethoven's time, a second set of tests was done on other skull bones from the same period. Beethoven's bones showed much higher concentrations, proving that his situation was unusual.

But if lead poisoning was the culprit in Beethoven's death, where did the lead come from?

There are a number of theories. Beethoven often drank from a favourite ceramic goblet, and there is speculation that the goblet may have been made with lead. In Beethoven's time, sugars containing lead particles were sometimes used to sweeten wine; this might have been another source of the poison.

Some scientists believe medical treatment Beethoven received at the end of his long illness could have contributed to his death. Beethoven's doctor in his final four months was Andreas Wawruch. To reduce the pain and swelling in Beethoven's stomach, Wawruch prescribed vast doses of salts for him to swallow. They had little effect. The swelling increased and when breathing became almost impossible, Wawruch tried more desperate measures. He pierced Beethoven's stomach and lungs with a lancet and drained the fluid. To ease Beethoven's pain and prevent infection, he patched the wound with a specially prepared healing mixture. Still Beethoven's condition worsened and his agony deepened.

Wawruch's treatment, some believe, may have been the final factor in Beethoven's death. As was often the case in Beethoven's day, the salts the composer swallowed might have contained lead. The healing mixture, too, may have been infused with high concentrations of lead compounds. These would have seeped through Beethoven's open sores and into his body, making his condition worse rather than better. In attempting to cure Beethoven, Wawruch's treatment might have actually pushed the composer's already weakened liver over the edge.

Whatever the exact cause of Beethoven's illness, lead poisoning seems to be a factor. It would explain his symptoms — mood swings, severe depression, gnawing stomach pains and perhaps even his deafness. The true marvel in Beethoven's story, however, is that despite his ailments the composer was able to work at all. Yet he did. During his lifetime, Beethoven composed hundreds of concertos, overtures, operas, symphonies and sonatas. So respected is Beethoven that even today, almost two centuries after his death, he is still considered to be one of the greatest of all composers.

The Case of the Intertwined Bones

Tucked away in a field in France, workers found two skeletons, their limbs overlapping. Who were they and why were they buried together?

On October 31, 2003, bulldozers and backhoes chewed up the earth outside Avion, France, preparing a field for a new gas pipeline. Amid the grind and growl of machinery, a discovery was made. Tucked under the soil, workers found human bones. Most were brown and weathered. A number of them were pitted and splintered. There were objects near the bones, too — lumps of metal, small buttons, bits of rubber, canvas and leather.

Construction was halted. Local police were called. The bones were extracted and examined. There were two skeletons, the bones intertwined, limbs criss-crossed and overlapping.

Because of the apparent age of the bones and the objects buried with them, investigators decided they were most likely soldiers who had died in World War I. Although the discovery was a surprise, it wasn't completely unexpected. During World War I, the field had been a battle site. Trenches had once riddled the area, providing cover and protection for German soldiers as Allied forces tried to reclaim the captured territory.

After most battles, the bodies of dead soldiers were retrieved, identified and given proper burials. Relatives at home were notified. Sometimes, though, identification was impossible. Occasionally, the enemy rounded up the dead and hastily buried the bodies in unmarked graves. Other times, the dead remained where they had fallen, mired in muck or covered by earth from bomb blasts. They became the missing — soldiers who never made it home and whose relatives were left wondering what happened to them.

Artifacts recovered with the bones at Avion included a tattered gas mask, water bottle, collapsible shovel, hand grenades, buckles, buttons, a button-cleaning kit, .303 ammunition and a dental plate containing six teeth. Most revealing were shoulder flashes and a regimental cap badge bearing the inscriptions *49* and *Canada*.

Canada's Department of National Defence was contacted. Immediately an investigation was launched to unravel the mystery of the unknown soldiers.

Since Canada still has 19,600 unidentified and missing soldiers from World War I, pinpointing the names of the men would be a challenge. Historian Dr. Ken Reynolds of the Directorate of History and Heritage (DHH) was consulted. Reynolds searched archives and databases. He found that the 49th Battalion had fought near Avion in June and July 1917. After a night raid on German trenches on June 8, 1917, thirty-six men had died. Sixteen bodies were never recovered.

The names of the sixteen missing soldiers were enshrined on the Vimy Memorial in France. From personnel records, Reynolds prepared summaries of the men, listing their ages at death, height, weight, medical condition and next of kin.

Two forensic anthropologists, Dr. Vera Tiesler-Blos and Dr. Carney Matheson, flew to Beaurains, France, where the remains were stored. It took about six hours to separate the bones into two sets. Both skeletons were incomplete. One was without lower limbs entirely.

The bones were measured, weighed and examined for signs of damage or injury. Teeth were studied for wear and decay. Profiles of both individuals were prepared. One was thought to be between twenty-six and thirty-four years old, 170 centimetres to 175 centimetres tall and, judging by the shape and condition of the bones, accustomed to physical labour. The second soldier had been slightly shorter and younger — aged twenty to twenty-five. This man appeared to have led an active and athletic lifestyle.

The physical profiles were compared to the list of sixteen unidentified soldiers prepared by Reynolds. Four matched the size, age and background of one of the skeletons. Five matched the other. The list of possibilities was now shorter — down to nine men.

To further narrow the list, Matheson extracted DNA from the two sets of remains and conducted tests to isolate their components. Meanwhile, Janet Roy, a genealogist, began the time-consuming task of tracing the next of kin of the nine men. She prepared a spreadsheet of the missing soldiers and listed their statistics — height, age, weight, occupation, birthplace and next of kin.

Using birth, death, marriage and census records as well as information from community and newspaper archives, Roy traced the living relatives of the men and mailed DNA swab kits to those who agreed to be tested. Her directions were specific: swab the inside of one cheek; let the swab dry for an hour and mail the sample back to the lab.

In the lab, Matheson compared the DNA of the two soldiers to the samples provided by relatives. He found a match to one of the names on the list. Private Herbert Peterson, a soldier from rural Alberta, had gone missing in France on June 8, 1917. His DNA matched his nephew's, another Herbert Peterson who lived in British Columbia.

Ninety years after he had been killed, Private Peterson was finally identified.

Private Herbert Peterson died on June 8, 1917, near the village of Avion, France. His name was carved onto the Vimy Memorial (above, left), along with those of 11,285 unknown Canadian soldiers who died in France. His remains were found eighty-six years later.

Pinpointing the identity of the other soldier proved more difficult. DNA erodes over time, and little of the second man's DNA material was usable. Scientists resorted to other methods. "You don't just use one tool," forensic expert Laurel Clegg explained. "You try to use as many tools as you can."

In the case of the second soldier, two tools proved helpful. One was stable isotope technology. Stable isotopes are elements that have an abnormal number of neutrons in their nucleus. They are found in soil and water, with the types and amounts varying from one geographical region to another. Isotopes are absorbed into the food chain, and as people consume food and water, isotopes are deposited in their teeth. By comparing the amounts of an isotope to levels of the same isotope found in different regions and countries, scientists can determine where a person once lived.

Since the front teeth are the first to develop, they are a permanent record of the first two years of life. The back teeth, which develop afterward, provide information about later years. In the case of the second soldier, the isotopes in his teeth were especially telling. They indicated that the soldier had been raised in Ireland. As a young man, he had immigrated to Canada and settled in southern Alberta. Only one missing soldier had the same history.

The second tool used by forensic experts was 3D skull reconstruction. Using the recovered skull and jawbone, forensic artist Christian Corbet reconstructed the soldier's likeness and sculpted a clay model of the head. A young man's face emerged, a perfect match to photographs of the soldier who had been identified by isotope technology.

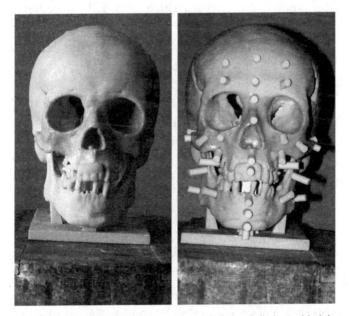

Artist Christian Corbet first made a resin model of the skull, then added tissue plugs as part of the facial reconstruction.

In January 2011, DHH released the findings. The second soldier was twenty-eight-year-old Private Thomas Lawless, an Irish immigrant who had settled in the Calgary area.

Although the two unknown soldiers have been identified, several questions remain unanswered. What happened those final moments in the trenches on the night of June 8, 1917? How did the two men end up in the same grave?

Scientists and historians have explored a number of possibilities. After the raid on the German trenches, German stretcher parties collected the wounded and dead for the next three days. It is possible that the bodies of the two Canadians were recovered by the Germans and given a hasty field burial. Also possible is that the two men were fighting near each other and the bomb that killed them threw their bodies together.

Another theory exists, too. Those familiar with wartime tactics say that under fire, soldiers crawl and keep low to the ground. Lawless's lower limbs were missing; Peterson's were chipped and splintered, but largely intact. It is possible that Lawless was carrying an injured Peterson. As the two men neared a German trench, an overhead shell might have exploded, blasting a hole in the ground, and throwing the men into the newly formed crater. The injuries suffered by the two soldiers are consistent with this act. One soldier standing in full view, carrying the other, would have received the brunt of the explosion; the man on his shoulders, less so.

The two soldiers, bound by death in battle, now rest in separate graves, just a couple of kilometres from the battlefield where they lost their lives. In 2007, accompanied by full military honours, Private Herbert Peterson was interred in La Chaudière Military Cemetery near Vimy, France. In 2011, Private Thomas Lawless was interred in the same cemetery, not far away from his companion.

Scientists Find the Answers

- *Why did dinosaurs die while other animals survived?*
  While dinosaur fossils are common in parts of Alberta, finding fossils of other animals that lived at the same time is rare. The 2010 discovery of a prehistoric graveyard near Hilda, Alberta, that contained thousands of bones of *centrosaurus,* a horned plant-eating dinosaur, helped scientists to explain why. Eons ago, much of southeastern Alberta was subject to frequent tropical storms and hurricanes. Paleontologists speculate that during such extreme events, lowland areas would become flooded. In the rapidly rising waters, creatures' size and speed mattered. Too bulky and slow to flee to higher ground, dinosaurs like the weighty *centrosaurus* drowned. Lighter, faster animals such as birds, reptiles and mammals, escaped and survived.

- *How do bees fly?*
  For years, scientists struggled to explain one of nature's curiosities: the flight of the honeybee. Considered too bulky and aerodynamically unsound to fly, the insect's ability to stay aloft was a mystery. In 2006, flight biologists at the California Institute of Technology filmed bees in flight, analyzed their movements and then built and tested flying robots equipped with sensors to mimic their actions. The explanation for the honeybee's gravity-defying ability? Rapid wing beats. Compared to smaller fruit flies, which beat their wings 200 times per second, the larger honeybee flaps its wings 230 times every second.

- *Why did the lake water turn red?*

When the Seealpsee, a mountain lake in Switzerland, suddenly turned blood red in July 2009, environmentalists were alarmed. Were there contaminants in the water? Microbiologists from Switzerland and Denmark took samples and analyzed the chemical and biological components of the water. The unusual red colour, they found, came from the sudden growth or "bloom" of a rare type of single-celled algae called *Tovellia sanguinea*. Just why the algae multiplied at such a rapid rate is under investigation, but some researchers theorize that nutrients from surrounding farms seeped into the water. Combined with ideal temperature and light conditions, the nutrients jump-started the algae's reproductive cycle.

CHAPTER 4
RESOLVE

Introduction

In 1815, the defeated French emperor Napoleon Bonaparte was exiled to the island of St. Helena by the English. After a lingering illness, he died in 1821. Officially, stomach cancer was given as the cause, but from the start conspiracy theories began circulating that Napoleon had been poisoned. The rumours were fuelled by something Napoleon had written two months before his death: "I am dying before my time, murdered by the English oligarchy and its hired assassins."

In 2001, it seemed that scientists had finally resolved the controversy. Tests done on a lock of Napoleon's hair that had been preserved by his valet showed high concentrations of arsenic. The poison was distributed along the shaft of the hair, not just the root, which suggested that the emperor had received a series of heavy doses over the four months before his death. It was believed Napoleon had been poisoned after all, although just how the poison had been administered or who had given it was uncertain.

Another study was conducted in 2002. French forensic experts examined strands of hair taken from Napoleon in 1805, 1814 and 1821. Again they found abnormally high levels of arsenic. But the researchers disagreed with the conclusions from the earlier study.

Based on their evidence, they concluded that Napoleon could not have been poisoned. As one scientist explained, "If arsenic caused Napoleon's death, he would have died three times over."

In 2007, an international team of pathologists examined autopsy reports prepared by Napoleon's doctor as well as several of the emperor's artifacts, including his pants. The autopsy report mentioned that a large tumour, approximately 10 centimetres in length, was found in Napoleon's stomach. When the researchers measured the pants, they noticed a trend. In the last six months of his life, Napoleon had lost roughly 10 to 15 kilograms. The size of the tumour coupled with Napoleon's large weight loss suggested that the original cause of death — stomach cancer — might have been correct.

But have science detectives actually resolved, once and for all, the question of Napoleon's death? What new insights or data will surface in the years to come that might change their answer?

As the Napoleon case and others in this chapter illustrate, scientific conclusions can change over time. Armed with new technologies and fresh approaches, scientists have the opportunity to settle long-standing questions. Was an Egyptian pharaoh murdered? Is a painting labelled a forgery actually a genuine masterpiece? Was a boy convicted of murder really innocent, as he claimed? With new evidence and ideas, conclusions can change, wrongs can be corrected and sometimes history may even have to be rewritten.

The Case of the Pharaoh's Suspicious Death

The boy king seemed to have been in the prime of his life, attractive and energetic, too young and vibrant for such an early death.

On the morning of November 4, 1922, after more than six years searching in Egypt's Valley of the Kings, Egyptologist Howard Carter ordered his workers to remove an ancient hut that stood on the dig site. Beneath the hut, the workers discovered a step. That step led to others — twelve in all — ending at an underground doorway. At the bottom, Carter broke a small hole in the door, and shone a light inside. A telegram he later sent to his benefactor in England, Lord Carnarvon, captures the thrill of what he saw: *At last have made wonderful discovery in valley; a magnificent tomb with seals intact; re-covered same for your arrival; congratulations.*

Magnificent, it was! Carter had found a room filled floor to ceiling with hundreds of beautiful objects: chariots overlaid with gold, elegant couches and gold-lined chairs, life-size statues adorned with jewels and gold, and dozens of toys, ornaments, vases, dishes and other vessels. But that room was just the beginning of marvellous surprises. Further into the tomb, Carter found a burial chamber containing a series of coffins, one inside the other. In the innermost coffin, made entirely of gold, he found the most valuable treasure of all — the mummified body of the young pharaoh, Tutankhamun.

Carter's discovery created an interest in Egyptian antiquities and burial practices that continues to this day. It also left some unanswered questions, a disturbing mystery and endless speculation.

Some of the questions centred around Tutankhamun's lineage and the boy king's place in Egypt's long and complicated history. His tomb was filled with riches, but by comparison, Tutankhamun's contributions to Egypt during his short reign seemed insignificant. He ruled for just nine years during the eighteenth dynasty of the New Kingdom. Little was known about Tutankhamun's parents or grandparents, his siblings, if he had children, how he came to inherit the throne or what he had accomplished before he died in 1324 B.C.

Equally mysterious was the manner of his death. Tutankhamun was just nineteen years old when he died. Artifacts in the tomb — the gilded statues, the golden masks — show a young man in the prime of his life, attractive and energetic, too young and vibrant for such an early death. From the moment of Carter's discovery of the tomb, Tutankhamun's death seemed suspicious.

The suspicions were fuelled by gaps in what was known about Egyptian history and by a string of odd coincidences, including the bizarre death of Lord Carnarvon a few months after the tomb's discovery. Other deaths followed. By 1934, six of the twenty-four people present at the official opening of the tomb had died. Rumours of a curse on the tomb began to circulate, giving Tutankhamun's death an even more sinister edge.

In 1968, scientists from the University of Liverpool in England X-rayed Tutankhamun's mummy. Ten years later, a research team from Michigan did the same. Unusual bone fragments were found inside the skull. Tutankhamun's leg appeared to be broken, and there was a wound on one cheek. Also startling was the discovery that his breastbone and front ribs were missing.

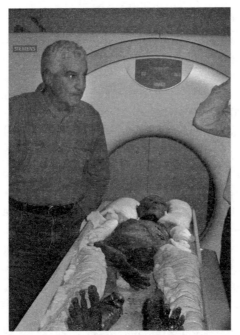

Zahi Hawass, leader of the Egyptian scientific team, supervises
the CT scan of the 3300-year-old mummy of Tutankhamun,
in an attempt to discover the cause of his early death.

The X-rays raised the suspense another notch. Had the boy king suffered a violent death, a crushing blow and other injuries that ended his life?

In 2005, experts in radiology, forensics and anatomy from Egypt, Italy and Germany embarked on a fresh study of Egyptian mummies. Rather than relying on artifacts for information, they applied the latest forensic tools to Tutankhamun and fifteen other mummies to determine the relationships between them, and the causes of their deaths.

In one part of the study, DNA tests were conducted. DNA

material was removed from the body by embalmers before the funeral; genetic markers were identified, tracked and compared.

In a second part of the study, a CT scan was done. On the evening of January 5, 2005, once tourists had left and the Valley of the Kings was closed to the public, Tutankhamun's mummy was carefully removed from its tomb. Workmen carried it up a ramp and a flight of metal stairs to a hydraulic lift where it was raised and loaded into a trailer that held a portable CT scanner. Seventeen hundred X-rays of the mummy were taken, each providing different digital images of thin-slice sections of the body. Stitched together by a computer, the scans would create a 3D view — a virtual body of Tutankhamun.

Less than three hours later, the scans were complete. Egypt's most famous mummy was returned to its tomb and safely laid in the sand-filled wooden tray that Carter had had specially built for it. The next day, visitors filed into the tomb, unaware that science had taken a giant step forward into solving an age-old puzzle.

Months later a report was issued that gave the results of the analysis. An entirely new picture of the boy king and the events surrounding his death emerged.

Guided by the CT model, measurements taken of the mummy and carvings found in the tomb, French anthropological sculptor Elisabeth Daynes produced a model of Tutankhamun's head. Working with similar data, Egyptian and American teams created their own versions. While different in some respects, the recreations show similarities, too — a teenager with an elongated skull, handsome in many ways, yet with imperfections, like a cleft palate and an overbite.

About 1.7 metres tall, Tutankhamun had been slightly built. Although apparently well nourished, he had been frail and suffered from several disorders. He had a club left foot, a flat right foot and had inherited a degenerative bone condition that likely affected his immune system, making him prone to disease. Tutankhamun might have walked with a stoop, probably in pain, and perhaps needed the assistance of a cane, which would explain the 130 walking sticks found in the tomb.

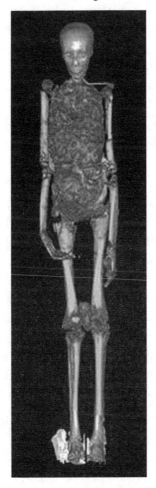

A CT scan of King Tut's mummy indicates that he was not murdered, but may have suffered a badly broken leg shortly before his death.

The CT scan detected fragments in the skull similar to those found in the 1968 X-ray. Closer examination, though, showed that they were hardened clumps of embalming resin, not chips of bone as originally thought. The discovery debunked the earlier theory: death was not the result of a crushing blow to the head.

So what was the cause? The scans showed a fractured left thigh bone and evidence of possible fractures to the right kneecap and right lower leg. Embalming fluid was found inside the left-thigh wound, suggesting that since the fracture still hadn't healed at the time of death, an accident must have happened shortly before.

DNA testing showed another curiosity. Tutankhamun and three other mummies showed signs of malaria. In ancient Egypt, malaria was a common illness, which sometimes leads to death.

By piecing together all the clues, scientists now figure that a rare combination of conditions likely caused Tutankhamun's death. Frail and carrying a genetic bone disease, the young king was in a weakened state. In the ninth year of his reign, he fractured his leg, opening the door to infection. When malaria-carrying mosquitoes transmitted the disease to him, his defenses were already down. Unable to fight the infection, Tutankhamun died.

"His weak bones made him a sick man," Zahi Hawass, leader of the Egyptian scientific team, explained. "The leg fracture coupled with the severe malaria made him die. He was not murdered."

CONTROVERSIAL
The Footprint Trail

In 1976, a fossilized footprint trail was discovered at Laetoli, Tanzania, by a team of scientists led by anthropologist Mary Leakey. Embedded in the rock-hard surface were two parallel sets of human-like footprints — one set large, the other small, a total of seventy footprints that ran more than 25 metres. The footprints had been made by hominids — creatures that stood upright and walked on two legs. At 3.6 million years old, the Laetoli footprints were the oldest hominid footprints ever found.

The discovery immediately sparked interest and controversy. Many scientists, Leakey included, believed that modern humans had evolved over time. Our ancestors, they argued, were early hominids similar to those that once lived around Laetoli. To these scientists, the footprints were clear evidence that early humans could walk on two legs long before they began to make and use tools or had developed fully functioning brains.

Other scientists have not accepted this argument. Any hominid skeletons unearthed so far bear little resemblance to human ones, they say, and because tools or weapons from the same period have not been found with the footprints, there is no proof that the Laetoli creatures have any human connection at all.

The debate about our human origins continues.

The Case of the Tarnished Lady

The painting was billed as a genuine Dutch masterpiece.
But art experts had been fooled before.

Crowds packed Sotheby's Art Auction House in London, England, on July 7, 2004. On the auction block that evening was a small painting, barely the size of a comic book cover. The painting showed a young, dreamy-eyed woman in a flowing gown sitting at a type of harpsichord called a virginal.

A Young Woman Seated at the Virginal was advertised as the first painting by famous Dutch artist Johannes Vermeer to come to auction in more than eighty years. Britain's Queen Elizabeth owned a Vermeer painting. The others were in public museums or galleries.

But was the "Lady" truly a Vermeer, or just a clever forgery? The painting had a troubled history and its authenticity had been questioned before. In fact, *all* Vermeer paintings had once been the subject of a long investigation. Thanks to one devious criminal, science had been called to reveal the truth in not just one case, but two now.

Case #1: Van Meegeren Strikes

Han van Meegeren was an artist who lived in the Netherlands in the first half of the twentieth century. As a painter he was not highly regarded or very successful. In fact, his work was widely scorned. Of van Meegeren, one critic wrote the stinging words, "he has every virtue except originality."

To get even with the critics, van Meegeren hatched a wild scheme. He would paint a perfect fake, one that mimicked a well-known artist's style so closely that even experts could not tell the difference. Once the fake painting had passed the inspection of experts and had been verified as genuine, van Meegeren would reveal the truth. He would show the experts to be fools, and have his revenge.

Van Meegeren chose to fake the work of Johannes Vermeer, a Dutch artist from the seventeenth century who had a unique style. An expert with light and shadow, Vermeer favoured bright colours, and applied paint in thin layers to give his subjects depth and texture. While other artists used common pigments, Vermeer often added dabs of expensive blue and yellow to highlight key areas.

In 1932, van Meegeren set to work. For six years, he experimented with various techniques. Finally confident that he had mastered Vermeer's method, he painted an entirely new subject — a painting he called *Disciples at Emmaus.*

As van Meegeren hoped, the painting passed the scrutiny of critics. One reviewer wrote, "We have here . . . I am inclined to say . . . the masterpiece of Johannes Vermeer of Delft." To great public acclaim, the painting was displayed in a prestigious gallery. Buyers jostled for position, eager to possess the newly discovered painting. It sold for the equivalent of what would now be several million dollars.

The public attention — and the great sum of money — went to van Meegeren's head. Rather than reveal the hoax, he decided to paint another "original" Vermeer. When that sold for an outrageous amount, he painted another. Then another. Seven Vermeer fakes in all.

But then the Nazis rose to power in Europe and confiscated many great works of art. Paintings by famous masters like Vermeer were in high demand. No one seemed to question why so many Vermeers were suddenly available or why van Meegeren was able to supply them. His forgeries sold quickly and for huge sums. Even Nazi field marshal Hermann Goering, Hitler's right-hand man, became a van Meegeren customer. For one of van Meegeren's "originals," Goering traded two hundred Dutch paintings that had been confiscated during the war. In the end, this would be van Meegeren's undoing.

To save his life, van Meegeren confessed to his scheme. *I am not a collaborator,* he told the court. *I couldn't be. I forged the painting myself.*

After World War II, suspected Nazi collaborators were arrested and brought to trial. Among the works of art discovered in Goering's personal collection was the Vermeer supplied by van Meegeren. Van Meegeren was charged with collaborating with the Nazis, a crime punishable by death. To save his life, van Meegeren confessed to his scheme. I am not a collaborator, he told the court. I couldn't be. I forged the painting myself.

To prove he was innocent of the collaboration charge, van Meegeren painted a fresh fake in front of witnesses, using the same methods he had used on the others. The new painting — *Jesus Amongst the Doctors* — looked like the genuine thing. But while the demonstration showed that van Meegeren was capable of painting a forgery, it did not prove that the painting he had supplied Goering was a fake.

The painting Goering had possessed was examined by a team of forensic scientists headed by Dr. Paul Coremans of the Central Laboratories of the Belgian Museums. Using a binocular microscope, the crackles — tiny cracks produced when paint dries — were magnified and examined. Most of the crackles looked old and genuine, but others looked fake. When X-rays of the painting were taken, the reason became apparent. Paint had been applied over another, older layer and had not penetrated through to the canvas.

Additional X-rays revealed that there was another, much-older painting underneath. Furthermore, the canvas was covered with five layers of paint, not the three that Vermeer traditionally used. When the paint was examined under a microscope, scientists detected diamond-shaped blue crystals, a distinctive feature of a synthetic pigment called cobalt blue. Since cobalt blue wasn't manufactured until the nineteenth century, it meant the painting could not have been produced in Vermeer's time.

The forensic examination proved van Meegeren's claim — the painting was a fake. In addition, the examination confirmed that the method van Meegeren used was the same as the one he had used to paint *Jesus Amongst the Doctors* in front of witnesses. Starting with an old painting, van Meegeren had scraped off most of the paint, taking care to leave a network of authentic crackles behind. Using specially prepared paints that contained a plastic bonding agent, he then painted a new image over top. To dry the paint, he baked it in a specially constructed oven. When the painting was dry, van Meegeren rolled up the canvas to enhance its crackled appearance.

The scientific investigation backed van Meegeren's story. The charge of corroboration was dismissed . . . though van Meegeren was found guilty of forgery instead. On November 12, 1947, he was sentenced to one year in prison. It was a sentence he never served. Barely a month later, van Meegeren died.

Case #2: The "Woman" in Question

Because of van Meegeren's crime, doubt was cast on other Vermeers. In 1948, an art expert published a book that listed all genuine Vermeers. There were only thirty-five in existence.

One well-known painting had been left off the list — a 25 by 20 centimetre painting of a lady seated at a virginal. Later the art expert changed his mind. *A Young Woman Seated at the Virginal* should have been included, he decided. He vowed that in the next edition of the book, he would correct the mistake. But there were no further editions and by now the damage had been done. The small painting's reputation was tainted. Doubt had been cast and the value of the painting plummeted.

For decades, *A Young Woman Seated at the Virginal* languished in controversy. Some art experts believed the painting was genuine; others swore it was a fake. One of the believers was its owner, Belgian art collector Baron Frederic Rolin. In 1993, he asked Sotheby's in London to investigate the work and settle the question.

For the next ten years, an international panel of scholars, museum curators, costume experts and forensic scientists studied the painting. It was carefully cleaned to expose its true colours. Using microscopes, each dab of colour and every brush stroke was examined in minute detail. X-rays were taken to show the underlying layers and how the paint had been applied. At the same time, historians investigated the painting's history to trace its origins and previous owners.

Signs that the painting was genuine soon appeared. The canvas, restorers discovered, was a close match to the one that had been used for *Lacemaker*, a Vermeer painting that hung in the Louvre in Paris. The brush strokes and the way the paint had been applied in thin layers matched genuine Vermeers, too.

To examine the pigments without damaging the painting, investigators used a method called Raman microscopy.

The most convincing proof, however, was in the paint itself. To examine the pigments without damaging the painting, investigators used a method called Raman microscopy. By shining non-destructive laser beams at the painting and measuring the reflected rays, they were able to detect changes in frequency between incoming and outgoing light. Since each chemical shifts light in a different way, scientists were able to identify the composition of the pigments in the painting by comparing the measured shifts to the frequencies of known substances.

Two colours stood apart from the others — yellow and blue. The yellow was identified as lead tin yellow, a colour widely used until the end of the seventeenth century, when it was replaced by other shades of yellow. The blue was identified as lazurite, an intense, brilliant hue so expensive that Vermeer only used it sparingly to accent small areas of his paintings. Lazurite was made from lapis lazuli, a semi-precious stone found in a remote mountain valley in Afghanistan, making it an extremely rare pigment choice and a difficult one to secure.

Because Vermeer was almost the only seventeenth-century artist to use both lead tin yellow and lazurite in his paintings, the presence of both pigments in the same painting identified it conclusively as genuine. *A Young Woman Seated at the Virginal* was the real thing, a true Vermeer. There was no doubt any longer.

A Young Woman Seated at the Virginal by Johannes Vermeer
is auctioned at Sotheby's in central London in 2004, for £16.2 million.

At Sotheby's Art Auction House, bidding on the "Woman" was fierce. The chance to own a real Vermeer — the thirty-sixth known Vermeer in existence — pushed up the painting's value. Experts predicted it would sell for about $5 million, but when the gavel finally came down, a new record had been established. Sold to an undisclosed buyer, *A Young Woman Seated at the Virginal* sold for £16.2 million — nearly $39 million.

TOOLS

Frequency

Visible light travels in waves and is a composite of seven main colours — red, orange, yellow, green, blue, indigo and violet. Each colour has unique wave properties. One of these properties is frequency: the number of waves that pass a point in a specified period of time. The colour red, for example, has a low frequency. The colour violet, on the other hand, has a higher frequency. The frequency of green is somewhere in between.

The Case of Death's Forgotten Visitor

Steven Truscott claimed he was innocent, but had he really killed twelve-year-old Lynne Harper? It took almost fifty years for science to find out.

In the Steven Truscott case, time was everything.

Around 7 p.m. on a hot evening in June 1959, fourteen-year-old Steven Truscott gave Lynne Harper a ride on the handlebars of his bicycle. As they pedalled north along a well-travelled road near the air force base outside Clinton, Ontario, the pair passed friends, classmates and several other witnesses. At 8 p.m. the same night, Truscott was spotted alone. By 11:30 p.m., Lynne hadn't come home, so her worried father called police.

Steven Truscott as a teenager.

Two days later, Lynne Harper's body was found in Lawson's Bush, not far from the road where Steven Truscott and the girl had been seen together. She'd been strangled to death. At an autopsy conducted the same evening, the pathologist pinpointed

133

the time of death. Lynne Harper had been murdered between 7:00 p.m. and 7:45 p.m. on the evening of June 9, 1959, around the time she'd been seen with Truscott.

A day after the discovery of the body, Truscott was taken into custody. Although he denied involvement in the crime, he was charged with murder. Three months later, after a fifteen-day trial, the jury reached a decision after debating the evidence for less than six hours: Truscott was guilty. The teen was sentenced to hang for Lynne Harper's murder.

It seemed that justice had been served. A killer had been caught, convicted and sentenced, the case closed and settled, all in 114 days. No one suspected — least of all Truscott in his cell on death row — that it would take almost fifty years for a tiny piece of scientific evidence to answer the question: Had Steven Truscott really killed Lynne Harper?

A few months after Truscott was sentenced, doubts began to emerge. Until 1976 when it was abolished, the death penalty was a common punishment for first-degree murder in Canada, but at fourteen, Truscott was the youngest person ever to receive the sentence. To many Canadians, the death penalty for one so young seemed unduly harsh. Some questioned the rapid-fire nature of the arrest, the speediness of the trial and the lack of fingerprints and other solid evidence that would have conclusively connected the teen to the crime. In response to the public outcry, Truscott's sentence was changed from death by hanging to life in prison.

Imprisoned in Collins Bay Penitentiary in Kingston, Ontario, Steven Truscott served his sentence, staunchly maintaining his innocence. In 1969, ten years into the sentence, twenty-four-year-old Truscott was released on parole. A public figure wanting a private life, he assumed another identity. For three decades he lived in Guelph, Ontario, his whereabouts and past unknown except to a few. He married, had children, worked as a millwright and lived as normal a life as possible. But as the years passed, Truscott — still vowing his innocence — yearned for justice.

In 2000, Truscott emerged from seclusion and launched a long legal fight to clear his name. Four years later, believing there might have been a miscarriage of justice, the Federal Minister of Justice referred the case to the Ontario Court of Appeal for review.

Decades had passed since the murder. The case had grown cold. Some of the witnesses and experts had moved away. Others had died, including Dr. John Penistan, the original pathologist in the case.

Since the murder, science had evolved, however. New methods and technologies were available, particularly in the use of DNA to solve crimes. In April 2006, as the investigation into the Truscott case swung into high gear, permission was granted for the remains of Lynne Harper to be exhumed. Hope hinged on finding traces of DNA evidence on the body that might identify the killer. Unfortunately, with the passage of time, no DNA had survived to provide fresh clues.

The guilty verdict against Truscott had rested almost entirely on the estimated time of death determined by Penistan's autopsy. Based on the condition of the stomach's contents and the fact that food had not yet moved from the stomach into the small intestine, Penistan had established a narrow time frame for the murder — between 7:00 p.m. and 7:45 p.m. Plenty of witnesses had seen Truscott biking with Harper around then.

In the 1950s and 1960s, time of death was often established through observation rather than through solid measurements.

Pathologists based their estimates on comparisons to other cases. During the Harper autopsy, Penistan had removed a pint of undigested food, placed it in a jar and held it up to the light. From his many years of examining stomach contents in other autopsies, he arrived at a figure. The food *looked* as if it had been in the stomach less than two hours. Since Lynne Harper had finished dinner at 5:45 p.m., he estimated that she had been murdered between 7:00 p.m. and 7:45 p.m.

They found evidence that had been largely ignored at the original trial.

Modern-day science relies on concrete evidence — measurements, calculations, tests and experiments — to arrive at such figures. Because the stomach contents from the original autopsy were no longer available to examine, investigators reviewed the evidence presented at the 1959 trial, hoping that with more sophisticated scientific methods a more exact timeline for the murder might be established.

Hidden in the files and documents, they found evidence that had been largely ignored at the original trial. Tiny visitors had arrived at the death scene.

Within minutes of Lynne Harper's death, bluebottle blowflies arrived, drawn by the scent of blood, urine and death's distinctive gases. The female blowflies laid eggs. The eggs soon hatched. Tiny white maggots, also called larvae, emerged. Fuelled by an abundant food supply, the maggots grew quickly.

By the time searchers found the body in a wooded grove two days after she went missing, hundreds of maggots were well established. Some were almost 2 millimetres long and nearly into the second stage of their development.

At the autopsy that evening, Penistan noted the presence of maggots on the body. Although the insects were considered unimportant to the case, he collected some in jars and sent them to a Toronto laboratory. There, biologist Elgin Brown made notes about the sizes of larvae plucked from various parts of the body. Photographs of the maggots were taken. Brown also selected a few maggots, hoping to grow them to maturity.

At the 1959 trial, Penistan was one of seventy-four witnesses called to the stand. He explained to the jury how he estimated time of death by analyzing the stomach's contents. Penistan mentioned the maggots at the trial, but only in passing. Though blowflies are death's first responders, that fact had not been considered important by Penistan or most other scientists of the time. After the verdict, while Truscott waited on death row, the blowfly information — measurements, notes, photographs — was filed with evidence from the trial and largely forgotten.

On June 19, 2006, a panel of five judges with the Ontario Court of Appeal convened to hear testimony and examine fresh evidence. One of the experts called to the stand was Dr. Nicholas Diamant, a gastroenterologist at Toronto Western Hospital. Gastroenterologists study the digestive system and its diseases. Diamant testified that he had reviewed the stomach content evidence obtained at the autopsy. Since the murder, more has been learned about how the body digests food, the factors that influence digestion and the changes that occur inside the stomach after death.

Diamant disputed Penistan's earlier figures. He told the court that it takes longer than once thought for the stomach to empty after a meal, and that emotional distress can stop digestion for several hours. Diamant's testimony cast doubt on Penistan's time-of-death estimate. Diamant claimed that Harper may have been murdered later than Penistan had figured.

The panel was also told that Penistan might have been less convinced of the time frame than his original testimony suggested. Penistan had prepared three versions of his autopsy report, each with a different time of death. The first two reports were never presented as evidence. One of the reports suggested that Harper had died after 8 p.m., well after Truscott was seen alone. In a handwritten note composed after the trial, Penistan wrote that he had fretted over the decision and feared that he might have spoken too convincingly. In hindsight, he felt that the time frame might not have been as exact as he had led the court to believe.

Harper must have been killed hours later than previously thought.

Forensic entomologists Richard Merritt, Gail Anderson and Sherah VanLaerhoven were also called to testify. Bluebottle blowflies, these modern entomologists know, are like ticking clocks, reproducing and moving through stages of change at predictable rates. By measuring the bluebottle maggots in the photographs taken by Brown, the entomologists established that the maggots must have been newly hatched. Since bluebottles don't fly or lay eggs at night, the scientists concluded that Harper must have been killed hours later than previously thought. Had she died at the time Penistan estimated, the maggots would have been larger.

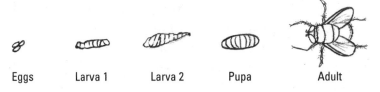

| Eggs | Larva 1 | Larva 2 | Pupa | Adult |

Scientists can determine time of death by the size of blowfly larvae on a corpse. Eggs to larva one = 23 hours; larva one to larva two = 49 hours; larva two to pupa = 130 hours; pupa to adult = 143 hours.

With testimony from modern scientists, a later time of death for the murder was established. Since Truscott was home by then, far from the scene, he couldn't have committed the crime.

On August 28, 2007, a verdict was reached. The forty-seven-year-old conviction was overturned. Although science could not identify the real murderer, Steven Truscott, at sixty-two years of age, was acquitted of the crime.

CONTROVERSIAL ▬▬▬▬▬▬▬▬▬▬

The Lindbergh Kidnapping and Murder

One of the most sensational crimes of the twentieth century was the 1932 kidnapping and murder of twenty-month-old Charles Lindbergh Jr., son of famed aviator Charles Lindbergh, the first person to fly solo non-stop across the Atlantic Ocean. After the baby was snatched from the second-storey nursery of the Lindberghs' New Jersey mansion in the dead of night, a ransom for his safe return was paid in marked bills. Two months after the kidnapping, the baby's body was found in a shallow grave. Several of the marked bills were eventually found in the possession of Bruno Hauptmann. Hauptmann was arrested, charged and brought to trial.

No identifiable fingerprints, footprints or tire marks had been found at the scene of the crime. Other than the ransom notes and two sections of a crude homemade wooden ladder that the kidnapper had used to climb to the second floor, there was little physical evidence.

National Forest Service scientist Arthur Koehler was called to examine the ladder. Koehler was a xylotomist, a scientist who studies growth patterns and cellular structures of wood. Koehler painstakingly took the ladder apart to examine each rung and rail. He was able to determine not only the mill where the wood had been processed and the machine that had planed it, but he was also able to show the jury that boards found in Hauptmann's attic were from the same batch and bore the same pattern of drilled holes as the ladder.

Based largely on Koehler's testimony, Hauptmann was found guilty. Although he maintained that he was innocent to the very end, Hauptmann was executed on April 3, 1936.

Since then, disturbing questions have been raised about the case. Although few dispute the science behind the conviction, some believe that the investigation was shoddy. Reporters and curious onlookers had swarmed the crime scene, leaving tracks, touching the ladder, and contaminating evidence. Sensing the public mood, the police were all too eager to make an arrest, and Hauptmann, a newcomer to the country, was an easy target.

To critics of the case, there are simply too many *ifs, maybes* and *could haves* to say without a doubt that Hauptmann was guilty. Questions linger and the debate continues. Was Hauptmann really the murderer? Or did an innocent man die in the electric chair?

Perhaps some day, with improved forensic methods, modern science will be able to settle the matter.

The Case of the Telltale Heart

Who had really died alone and wracked with disease in that prison cell during the French Revolution? Was it Louis-Charles, the rightful heir to the throne, or some unfortunate look-alike?

In 1789, with France facing economic ruin and widespread famine, mobs seized control of the country from King Louis XVI and his aristocratic followers. Between 1793 and 1794, in the period known as the Reign of Terror, public beheadings were a daily attraction. Accused of corruption and conspiracy, at least sixteen thousand aristocrats — perhaps as many as forty thousand — were guillotined. Others languished in prison, forgotten or ignored, their fate uncertain.

From this bloody page of history, a mystery emerged and a legend grew. King Louis XVI was executed on January 21, 1793. Ten months later, on October 16, Queen Marie Antoinette suffered the same fate. Their only living son, and heir to the French throne, eight-year-old Louis-Charles, was spared. Torn from his mother's side before her death, the frail boy was locked in a filthy, windowless cell in Paris's Temple Prison. Isolated, neglected and rarely seen, the future king died in the prison on June 8, 1795.

Upon news of the boy's death, a rumour that Louis-Charles was still alive — that a look-alike had died in his place — began to spread across France. Some people believed that with the help of loyal supporters, the real Louis-Charles had been smuggled out of prison. The boy was merely hiding, they thought, waiting until it was safe to reclaim the throne.

The rumour was fed by a lack of evidence. For much of

his imprisonment, the boy had been held in solitary confinement. The day after his death, a doctor had performed a hasty autopsy. He declared that Louis-Charles had died of tuberculosis. Without ceremony, the body was placed in a pine coffin and buried in a common grave in the cemetery of Sainte Marguerite in Paris, without even a stone or marker. Few had seen the boy while he was in prison. Fewer still had seen the dead body.

The possibility that Louis-Charles might have survived the Revolution spawned a parade of pretenders. More than one hundred people claiming to be the "real" Louis-Charles appeared, all laying claim to the throne. Among the many hopefuls were a poor stable boy, a German clockmaker and even a missionary from Green Bay, Wisconsin.

Ever since the French Revolution, the question of who died in the prison cell has been explored from many angles. In 1846, the burial site was secretly investigated by the abbé of Saint Marguerite. Below the surface, a 1.5-metre-long coffin was found. Inside was the rotting skeleton of a young boy, his skullcap sawn, his reddish-blond curls still clinging to the bone. The body had clearly been autopsied, and showed signs of disease. Both elements matched what would be expected for Louis-Charles. But the bones seemed too long for a ten-year-old. And the coffin was made of lead, not wood. Confused, and believing that the body was not that of Louis-Charles but an older teenager, the abbé reburied the remains in an oak coffin.

In 1894, a team of doctors and scientists re-investigated the grave. In front of journalists and other witnesses, the oak coffin was opened. The skull was examined, the bones measured, the teeth scrutinized. Again the results were baffling. The skeleton seemed to belong to a teenager at least fourteen years old. How could this be Louis-Charles?

In the 1970s other areas of the cemetery were searched, this time deeper and more extensively than before. Bits of bone were extracted. None of them seemed to come from a ten-year-old boy buried for almost two centuries. The body of Louis-Charles, if indeed there had ever been one, had disappeared, consumed by the earth and erased by time.

Without solid proof and facing conflicting evidence, the mystery deepened and the rumours continued. Perhaps Louis-Charles had escaped after all.

But one piece of proof had survived. For centuries it was tradition that upon death, the hearts of French kings would be removed from their bodies, embalmed and placed in the royal crypt at the Basilica of Saint Denis in Paris. At Louis-Charles's autopsy, Dr. Philippe-Jean Pelletan had followed this tradition. He had cut out the heart. Considering the dangerous times and the violent anti-royalist mood of the French Revolution, it was a daring move, one best kept secret. "I wrapped it in a handkerchief and put [it] in my pocket without being seen," Pelletan wrote later.

After smuggling the heart out of prison, Pelletan placed it in a jar, covered it with distilled wine alcohol to preserve it, and kept the heart out of sight on the top shelf of a bookcase. At one point, the heart was stolen from Pelletan. Later it was returned. In 1830, the glass jar broke during a scuffle and for a while the heart was lost. Days later it was located, partially buried in sand. In the two centuries that followed the Revolution, the pickled heart was neglected. The alcohol eventually evaporated and the organ dried, turning hard as leather.

An urn with the heart of Louis XVII was buried in June 2004, over two hundred years after his death in Paris's Temple prison.

For a time, the heart was kept and protected by descendants of the royal family. Finally, in 1975, it was donated to the Basilica of Saint Denis in Paris. Sealed in a crystal urn, the heart was placed on a shelf along the far wall of the family crypt. The two-hundred-year-old heart, wrinkled and brown, now had a permanent home.

Still, questions lingered and the old rumour refused to die. Was it really the heart of Louis-Charles, the rightful heir to the throne? Or was it the heart of another child? And if it was, what had really happened to Louis-Charles?

As the twentieth century closed, advances in DNA fingerprinting offered hope that the questions might finally be answered. On December 15, 1999, a small group of scientists, historians, journalists and others interested in the case gathered inside the royal crypt at the Basilica of Saint Denis. In the crowd was Philippe Delorme, a French historian. He had studied the heart's history, and could verify that it was the same organ as the one removed during the boy's autopsy in 1783. Also present was Jean-Jacques Cassiman, a Belgian professor of genetics and an expert on DNA fingerprinting.

The wrought-iron gate guarding the entrance to the crypt was unlocked. The sealed crystal urn was taken from the shelf. After a brief ceremony, it was carried to a hearse waiting outside and whisked through the streets of Paris to the Thierry Côté Medical Analysis Laboratory a few blocks away.

In front of witnesses, the seal was broken and the urn was opened. The heart was hard as rock, but remarkably intact.

Using a sterile handsaw, Cassiman cut along the bottom tip and removed a small strip, barely a centimetre wide. A sample of the aorta, the main artery coming from the heart, was also taken. The pieces were divided in two and placed in separate sterile tubes. One tube was sent to Ernst Brinkmann, a geneticist in Germany. The other tube was taken to Cassiman's laboratory in Leuven, Belgium.

The scientists focused on finding a match to the heart's mitochondrial DNA. While Brinkmann conducted independent tests on the heart material, Cassiman proceeded on his own. To begin, he cut the fragments of heart material into small pieces and crushed them into fine particles. Using special enzymes, the cellular material was dissolved and broken down. By using a newly developed technique known as PCR or polymerase chain reaction, Cassiman replicated tiny traces of the heart's mitochondrial DNA to produce a larger sample. Once this was done, the samples were placed in a machine known as a sequencer. It produced a readout of the heart's unique mitochondrial DNA sequence.

To determine if the heart really belonged to Louis-Charles, Cassiman compared the mitochondrial DNA of the heart to mitochondrial DNA taken from living and deceased maternal relatives of the lost king. Cassiman wrote to Queen Anne of Romania and her brother, André de Bourbon-Parme, both living descendents of Marie Antoinette. Queen Anne donated a sample of blood; her brother strands of hair. To obtain mitochondrial DNA from deceased relatives, Cassiman located preserved locks of hair that belonged to Marie Antoinette and two of her sisters.

The sequence produced a readout of the heart's unique DNA.

Although there wasn't enough DNA in Marie Antoinette's hair to use, the supply from her younger sister, Johanna Gabriela of Austria, was sufficient. When the mitochondrial DNA sequence of the heart tissue was compared to Johanna Gabriela's, there was a positive match. The sequence also matched the mitochondrial material obtained from Queen Anne and her brother.

Cassiman had discovered a genetic link between the heart and the maternal bloodlines of France's royal family. But before the results could be considered conclusive, one more important step had to be taken. Brinkmann had been conducting independent tests on the heart material in Germany. Could he verify that the mitochondrial DNA sequence of the heart was the same as the one found by Cassiman?

On April 3, 2000, Brinkmann and Cassiman met to compare their findings. Their mitochondrial sequences were identical. "Not only did we have sequence alignment . . . with living and deceased relatives, but we also had independent confirmation from another lab," Cassiman reported.

It was a historic moment. Science had ended over two hundred years of speculation. The heart belonged to Louis-Charles, the lost king of France. The unfortunate boy had not escaped. He had died alone in prison, wracked by disease, neglected and frightened. The one hundred men who had tried to claim the throne afterwards had all been imposters.

In 2004, European royalty gathered inside the Basilica of Saint Denis. Following a solemn ceremony, the heart of Louis-Charles, sealed now in a new urn, was laid to rest in its rightful place in the royal crypt near the graves of Marie Antoinette and Louis XVI, bringing to a final close two centuries of rumour, legend and mystery.

Scientists Find the Answers

- *Why do worms surface?*

  Hammer a wooden stake into the ground, rub the top of it with a metal rod to produce a grunting or snoring sound, and if conditions are just right, earthworms will race to the surface. Known as worm grunting, the practice posed a scientific mystery until 2008, when American neuroscientist Kenneth Catania conducted a series of experiments to find the answer. Suspecting that the vibrations mimicked those produced by moles — a natural predator of worms — Catania filled a box with dirt, added three hundred worms and then introduced a mole. Within an hour, one-third of the worms were at the surface. Sound frequency comparisons showed that sounds produced by worm grunting and digging moles were almost the same, adding further evidence to support Catania's hypothesis.

- *Do sharks need to mate?*

  In 2001, a hammerhead shark born at the Henry Doorly Zoo in Nebraska offered scientists a baffling puzzle. In the tank with the newborn pup were three other hammerheads, all females that had been in captivity for three years or more. Isolated from male sharks, none of them had mated. Under such circumstances, how was reproduction possible? In 2007, DNA tests of the pup and female sharks provided a surprising explanation. The DNA of one female matched the pup's DNA perfectly; no male had contributed to its DNA. The pup did not have a father, proving for the first time that in rare circumstances, female sharks can reproduce asexually (without partners) through a process known as parthenogenesis.

- *Where did Arctic peoples come from?*

  Thousands of years ago, before ancestors of the Inuit and other native peoples populated the northern regions of Greenland and North America, the areas were barren of people. Just how, when and why people migrated to the Arctic have been long-standing questions. In 2009, the DNA extracted from a tuft of four-thousand-year-old hair unearthed from Greenland's permafrost provided some answers. Analysis of the DNA showed that the hair came from a prehistoric male, a member of the Saqqua group that once lived in Siberia. While the discovery established the origins of at least one group of the Arctic's people, scientists have not yet determined why and how the Saqqua made the journey.

GLOSSARY

acoustical engineer: a specialist in sound and its properties.

aeronautics engineer: a specialist in the design, construction and safety of aircraft.

anatomy: a branch of science that studies the structure of living things.

anthropologist: a scientist who studies the development, behaviour and social practices of humans.

archaeologist: an anthropologist specializing in the study of people, cultures and civilizations from the past.

archives: a place or collection containing records, documents or other materials of historical interest.

artifact: an object made by humans, such as a tool, weapon or ornament.

astronomer: one who studies celestial bodies such as planets, stars and galaxies.

autopsy: the examination of a dead body, usually with a dissection, to determine cause of death.

biochemist: one who studies chemical compounds and reactions that occur in living organisms.

biologist: a scientist who studies living things.

chemist: a scientist who studies substances, their properties, and the ways they interact.

CT (computerized axial tomography) scan: a sophisticated X-ray technique that uses a computer to merge X-rays taken from several angles into a single 3D image; also called a CAT scan.

DNA (deoxyribonucleic acid): the molecule that contains the genetic information that tells cells how to grow and function.

entomologist: a scientist specializing in the study of insects.

epidemiologist: a medical specialist concerned with the transmission and control of epidemic diseases.

exhume: to remove a coffin and corpse from a grave.

forensics: the use of scientific methods and techniques, such as genetic fingerprinting, to solve crimes.

forensic pathologist: one who investigates the cause of death, usually for legal purposes.

frequency: the number of waves that pass a point in a specified period of time.

gastroenterologist: a doctor who specializes in the digestive system and its diseases.

gene: a segment of DNA that determines a particular characteristic.

genetic marker: a gene or DNA sequence that is linked to a specific trait, family feature or disease, and whose inheritance can be followed.

geologist: a scientist who studies the origin, history, structure and composition of the Earth.

ingot: metal that is cast into a convenient shape for shipping or trade.

isotope: an atom whose nucleus contains an abnormal number of neutrons.

medical artist: an artist who specializes in creating and interpreting medical and biological images.

microbiologist: a scientist who studies microscopic forms of life such as bacteria and fungi.

mitochondrial DNA: a type of DNA, found outside the nucleus of the cell, that is passed unchanged along the female line of the family and contains the genetic blueprint of only one parent, the mother.

MRI (magnetic resonance imaging): a procedure that uses powerful magnets and radio waves to construct computer pictures of the body's interior.

neuroscientist: one who specializes in the study of the nervous system.

paleontologist: a scientist who studies and interprets fossil remains of ancient plants and animals.

parthenogenesis: the process by which the female of a species is able to reproduce without a male.

pathologist: a doctor who specializes in the causes and development of diseases.

phrenology: a now abandoned theory that much about a person's personality and ability can be learned from the shape and size of the skull.

radioactive substance: a material that emits radiation — energy in the form of rays, waves or particles.

radiocarbon dating: a method of determining the age of organic substances by measuring the amount of radioactive carbon they contain.

radiologist: a medical specialist who creates and interprets pictures of areas inside the body using methods such as X-rays, CT scans, MRIs and ultrasound.

Raman microscopy: a method of analyzing the shift in frequency of reflected laser light to determine the chemical composition of a material.

refraction: the bending of light as it passes through substances such as glass or water.

skull-face superimposition: a method of matching skulls with faces by positioning photographs, video or computer-generated models over each other.

virologist: a scientist who studies or specializes in viruses.

X-rays: high-frequency electromagnetic waves that can penetrate certain substances, such as skin.

xylotomist: a scientist who studies growth patterns and cellular structures of wood.

INDEX

PHOTO CREDITS

...NLEDGEMENTS

...core, this book owes everything to the dedicated scientists, ...earchers and technicians mentioned in its pages. Although sometimes from different branches of the scientific tree, they are nevertheless driven by similar quests — the pursuit for answers to questions, the search for knowledge and understanding, the unravelling of life's mysteries. These common threads are at the heart of every story.

Behind the book, too, are educators — too numerous to list — who have sparked my curiosity and stretched my own understandings, both those who have taught me as well as those who have taught with me over the years. Their influence is etched on each of these pages.

I am also indebted to the team at Scholastic Canada who, driven by high standards, worked tirelessly to shape this book and hone the words. My sincerest thanks to editor Carrie Gleason, who saw promise in the raw material, asked probing questions, made valued suggestions, and kept the vision alive over the long haul. My thanks, too, to others who left their mark in significant ways, particularly Vice-President of Publishing Diane Kerner, Senior Editor Sandy Bogart Johnston, and Art Director Aldo Fierro.

Finally, to the many others in my life — family, friends, colleagues, students — who in ways profound and subtle, direct and indirect, encouraged, guided and inspired. I couldn't have done it without you. My heartfelt thanks.